BEE ALERT!

First published in Great Britain in 2018
Text © Barbara Rustin 2018
Illustrations © Josephine Birch 2018
The moral rights of the author have been asserted
All characters and events in this publication,
other than those clearly in the public domain,
are fictitious and any resemblance to real persons,
living or dead, is purely coincidental

No part of this book may be reproduced, stored in
a retrieval system, or transmitted, in any form or by any means,
without the prior permission in writing of the publisher or author,
nor be otherwise circulated in any form of binding or cover
other than that in which it is published and without a similar
condition including this condition being imposed
on the subsequent purchaser

ISBN 978-1-5272-1741-6

Printed and bound in Great Britain
by Clays Ltd

BEE ALERT!

Barbara Rustin
Illustrated by Josephine Birch

For
Nigel, our children and, particularly, our grandchildren,
Mayane, Samala, Isaac, Yuval, Eli, Max, Gil and Alexa
– BR

For
Wyn – JB

A
pessimist sees the difficulty in every opportunity;
an optimist sees the opportunity in every difficulty

Winston Churchill

Chapter One

Those girl detectives have all the luck when it comes to finding bodies, Ben was thinking to himself as he carefully made his way down the little staircase that led from his attic. *They always seem to be in the right place at the right time.*

Ben was planning to be a detective himself. He'd bought the latest Lulu and Lee, Leading Lady Detectives book to read while he stayed at Gramps's for the holidays. It was so gripping he'd nearly finished it on the train.

Lulu and Lee had been staying in a massive country house – a mansion really. They'd found the body in the library. How shocked they'd been when they'd opened the door and seen a bald man lying spreadeagled on the floor, an exotic oriental dagger plunged into his chest.

Ben sighed as he came down the main stairs and headed towards the kitchen. What chance of him having a crime like that to investigate? He thought of the houses around Gramps. They were mostly cottages. The largest house he could think of was Broadacres and although it was big it certainly wasn't a mansion. Anyway, Gramps hardly knew the Corbridges who owned it so, if anything exciting did happen there, he wouldn't be around.

Never mind. He was going to be here for five weeks. If he kept his eyes open, there was bound to be some crime or other in that time. A grin appeared on his face. Horse rustling – that was it! He'd just read somewhere or other that ten thousand horses are stolen every year.

He took the last few stairs at a jump, sniffing the air hopefully. Nothing. Strange. Why was there no smell of the Welcome Pancakes Gramps always made for his first breakfast?

Ben opened the kitchen door to find his grandfather sitting at the kitchen table, eyes fixed to the newspaper spread out in front of him, his uneaten toast cold and his coffee scummy. He barely looked up when Ben came in the kitchen.

'Hi, Ben. Help yourself to cereal,' was all he said.

He'd fixed a smile to his face, but his eyes were already sliding back to his paper.

Ben suddenly remembered a conversation he'd overheard a couple of weeks before the start of the holidays. 'I really can't understand you sending Ben down to Dad for the holidays. Don't know about "Gramps"; he's more like "Grumps" these days.'

His Auntie Lizzie had popped over to see his mum, and Ben, going past the sitting-room door, had paused when he'd heard his name. Well, it wasn't exactly eavesdropping, was it? They were speaking about him, after all, and, anyway, he was listening for professional reasons. As a detective,

you always had to be on the alert for information that might turn out to be useful.

'Let's face it, he's never been the same since Mum died,' his Auntie Lizzie had continued. 'All turned in on himself and not bothering with any of his friends. What fun is that going to be for Ben?'

'That's so unfair, Liz. Dad's not like that with Ben. Perks up when he's around. And it's great for Ben too, you know. He loves being in the countryside and he's much more mature when he's with Dad. Has he shown you *Ben's Bee Book* – the book Ben's been making when he stays there, by any chance?'

'Can't say he has.'

'Well, ask him to next time you're there. Honestly, it's worth looking at – full of all sorts of unusual facts Ben has picked up about bees. He's illustrated it too, with quaint little pictures he's found in some old book. ❂ I only wish he'd get involved in school projects like that. Heavens, you can't imagine the battles I've had just to get him to do his homework this year. And as for his report! Well, let's just not go there.'

Ben, behind the door, had felt his ears go pink. And had tiptoed away into the garden.

But maybe Auntie Lizzie did have a point about Gramps he thought now as he sat at the table contemplating the cereal packet – which was not even the super-extra-berries one that was his favourite – and feeling neglected.

He peered across the table at Gramps's newspaper. It wasn't easy to read it upside down across the table. Hey. Wasn't that word 'MYSTERY' in the headlines? Grandpa's hand was

covering the next bit, but the word after started 'COLL'. Yes, 'COLLAPSE' – that was it and then, 'DISORDER!' Dramatic stuff. No wonder Gramps was so engrossed.

'Your article looks exciting, Gramps.'

His grandfather looked at him for a moment. 'Not exactly the word I'd use, Ben.' His voice was flat. He sighed. 'It's about what's happening with bees.'

'Disorderly bees, Gramps? You can't mean it!'

'Bit complicated to explain, Ben, but I'll try.'

Ben, however, had just noticed the sun streaming in through the window. He looked out and saw raindrops sparkling in the grass. Last night teeming rain had prevented him going to look at the bees with Gramps. Usually it was the first thing he did when he arrived. He decided the explanation could wait.

'How about we get our bee kits on now? Yes, we should take advantage of the good weather,' he said, copying the expression his grandfather used when he was trying to lure Ben away from a video game. He grinned at Gramps.

But Gramps's face remained serious. 'Of course, Ben,' he said, 'but first . . .' He paused. His face was now scrunched up into a frown and his bushy eyebrows were joining over his nose like two furry caterpillars. 'Ben, I'm really sorry, but there's something I've got to tell you first. And it's not good news, I'm afraid.'

Ben's stomach did a lurching somersault. Oh no. Don't say it was Gramps who was really ill now. Since Gran had died of a heart attack two years ago, nothing in his life felt quite so solid. Horrible things could just happen with no warning.

'It's to do with the bees,' Gramps continued. He looked at Ben apparently completely unaware that his right hand was tightly holding the fingers of his left hand and was tugging away at them as if to pull them off. Ben was relieved, though, to hear that it was the bees and not his health that Gramps was worried about.

'I didn't want to upset you as soon as you arrived yesterday, but . . . oh, Ben, it's just awful.' He paused a moment, shaking his head helplessly, but before he could continue the phone interrupted him.

'Sorry, Ben, I won't be a sec,' he said, picking it up. 'Hello? Oh, hi, Chris, you got my message, then . . . No, no . . . Well, I didn't realise how serious it was then . . . half a dozen maybe . . . But now . . . Yes, complete catastrophe.'

There was a pause as Grandpa listened. Then suddenly his voice changed.

'Oh really, Chris, just don't start on that again . . .' There was another pause. Gramps's face was getting red. 'Look, you know what, Chris, I've heard just about enough about your blasted top bar hives . . .' He continued to splutter his indignation down the phone, apparently forgetting Ben's presence.

Ben sighed. So much for 'won't be a sec'. If Gramps and Chris were into one of their 'My Kind of Hives are the Best' arguments, they'd be at it for ages. They never usually got as heated as this!

Right. He'd just go and look by himself, then, and find out what was going on. After all, he'd never been frightened of bees. But, as he went out into the hall shutting the kitchen door quietly behind him, he felt his stomach starting to churn. Why was it doing that?

He couldn't suddenly be anxious about going into Gramps's field of hives by himself could he?

He realised that his grandfather's words were echoing in his head. 'Just awful . . . complete catastrophe.' What on earth had happened?

Chapter Two

Ben tore down the garden, past the large vegetable patch and on towards the field where Gramps had all his beehives. As he approached the gate, a horrible thought burst into his head. What if Grandpa's bad news was that the bees had turned angry and aggressive – like those terrifying African killer bees?

He slowed down. His legs had suddenly gone sort of watery and seemed unable to keep up the speed. And what about his protective clothing? Blast! He'd forgotten to put it on. He came to an abrupt halt.

Maybe I should go back, he thought. He looked around. Gramps's hives were dotted about the meadow as usual. It was all peaceful enough. There'd be an angry buzzing, surely, if the bees had turned nasty?

And that was when he realised. The meadow might look the same, but of course it wasn't. That magic moment of opening the gate whenever he came wasn't just to do with what he saw. It was all the other sensations that greeted

him at the same time – the grassy scent of the field, the busy hum of the bees in the warm air. But today the field was silent.

The bees had gone. Gosh, Grandpa had had tens of thousands of bees and now there wasn't a single one to be seen. For a few moments Ben couldn't move. The watery feeling was in his stomach now as he thought of what he might find. But curiosity got the better of him. He gripped his stomach muscles tightly as he set off towards the nearest group of hives. Would the ground around them be a black carpet of dead bees? But, no, there was nothing on the ground and all was eerily still.

As he was walking round the different hives searching for a

sign of life, he felt a gentle squeeze on his shoulder. 'Sorry, Ben. I had wanted to warn you before we came down here, but then Chris called and—'

'What on earth's happened to them, Gramps?'

'Well, that's it, Ben. They've totally disappeared and I haven't any idea why. Of course it's been happening not only in this country but all over the world. Yet I was still stupidly hoping that somehow mine would be safe. And I don't need to tell you—'

Grandpa stopped suddenly. No, he certainly did not need to explain to Ben how important bees were to humans. His grandson wasn't particularly keen on drawing, he knew, but when there had been a project at his school about pollination his poster had won the prize.

Ben stood twiddling his hair so that it stood up spikily as he eyed Gramps anxiously. He was worried about the bees, but also about how his grandfather was going to cope without his many colonies. He was never more cheerful than when he was busy with his hives. Gramps noticed his face.

'Ben,' he said quickly, 'there are a few hives that do still have their bees. Let's get our bee suits and do a quick check-up on them.'

Ben loved the shed near the house where his grandfather kept all his bee paraphernalia and protective clothing. When he was little, he'd thought Gramps looked like an astronaut in his white helmet and suit.

'Hey, do you remember how enormous this was on me last

THE IMPORTANCE of BEES

BEES

are covered in tiny hairs which pick up pollen from blossom and flowers. Then they transfer the pollen from a part of the plant called the ANTHER to the STIGMA.

This causes **POLLINATION** which means a **BIGGER and BETTER CROP**

LOTS OF VEGETABLES DEPEND ON BEES

WITHOUT BEES WE WOULDN'T HAVE,...

BEES also pollinate the crops that feed cattle so we wouldn't have...

year, Gramps.' he said as he put his own suit on. He'd been very excited when Grandpa had given it to him, but had been absolutely swamped in it. 'Look, fits me fine now.'

He picked up the smoke gun, his favourite piece of equipment, with his gloved hand. 'I'll take this, Gramps?' Gramps shut the shed door and they set off back to the field.

'What I don't understand, Gramps, is where they've all gone. I mean, usually if masses have died you see them lying all over the ground, don't you?'

'Right. And, though it's horrible to see them, at least then you know what you're dealing with – or you can guess what caused it. Remember what happened last time you were here?'

'Sure do. We found a load of dead bees and went straight round to see Farmer Fart,' said Ben, grinning. Gramps's eyes narrowed as he looked at him.

'Yes, we went to see Fred Bart,' he said, emphasising the B. 'He'd just sprayed his fruit trees, remember? Showed us the packet he'd used and claimed it couldn't harm bees or bugs, but what did I see in the corner of the package?'

'A picture of a skull and crossbones.'

Grandpa nodded. 'Precisely. We all know what that means don't we? No wonder I was angry. And if it's poisonous for humans, how much more deadly is it going to be for bees?'

'Well, you certainly were cross. Seem

to remember after we left you said he was a silly old fart.'

'Yeah, well, maybe I did mutter something like that, but it certainly wasn't meant for your donkey's ears. And Fred's never caused any problems since then.

'But you know, Ben, upsetting as it was to find all those bees dead, it wasn't as bad as this. With them disappearing without a trace, I feel so helpless. I have absolutely no idea what is going on or how to prevent it from happening again, you see.'

Ben stared at him silently. Even through the protective netting of his hood Gramps could see how anxious Ben's face was. This wasn't at all what he'd had in mind for the first day of his stay. 'Well now, how about finding something to fill the smoke gun?' he suggested.

Ben felt a bit happier as he gathered the pine needles lying on the ground around the trees. He loved the smell and knew they made loads of smoke as they burned.

'OK. You ready?' Gramps asked a few minutes later. Ben grinned to himself. He knew this was just Gramps's tactful way of reminding him to act calmly when they lit the gun and approached the hives. Bees got anxious themselves if they felt you were nervous or excitable.

'Yeah, I'm fine, Gramps.'

'Quite sure you don't want to stop here and have a go with the gun before we go into the field?' Gramps said, grinning. Ben laughed. When he'd been too young to use the gun near the hives, Gramps would light it and let him use it in the garden.

Great fun it had been, twirling around belching out smoke in all directions.

Recently Gramps had let him hold the smoking gun while they inspected the hives together. Although the bees didn't like the smoke, it distracted them and they were much less likely to sting.

'Okay. Let's go, then. I'll show you where the healthy hives are. And let's just hope they are still healthy.'

At the far side of the meadow was a clump of trees that hid a cluster of hives. As they approached, Ben heard the dense sound of bees humming. Then he saw the hives and the bees coming and going, specks of gold darting about in the air.

'Hey, these look in good shape, don't they, Ben? Let's have a closer look.'

Ben eagerly opened the gun. Gramps passed him the box of matches. Ben lit one and dropped it into the cylinder. In less than a minute the pine needles caught fire and started to smoke. Now for the best bit.

'You ready to open up, Gramps?'

'Yup.'

Ben squeezed the bellows and smoke poured out of the smoke gun. He directed the plume of smoke towards each of the four corners of the hive in turn.

'OK, Ben.' Gramps waited a moment or two then lifted the hive lid and took out a frame. It was heaving with bees, so many that the comb itself with its little hexagonal cells was almost completely covered with a thick, whirring mass of golden-brown bees.

'Wow, that looks good doesn't it, Gramps? I mean, there are

so many you just can't tell one from another or see what they're doing.'

'Yup, and the frame is really heavy so it must be full of honey. Look, you can just see some open cells with larva inside. The queen ✿ must be all right too because these could only have been laid a day or two ago. Nothing to worry about here, I'm glad to say. Now, do you want to have a closer look at one of the others?' He pointed back at the meadow where all the abandoned hives were standing.

An empty hive? Not very cheerful, Ben thought. But he was curious and it was an opportunity to use the gun. Walking back the way they had come, Ben noticed that not all the hives were totally empty. Some had a few bees lazily coming and going. He pointed to one of them.

'There is a sign of life in that one, Gramps.'

'Puff a bit of smoke around it and we'll see what's going on.' After a minute or two he lifted out a frame for Ben to see.

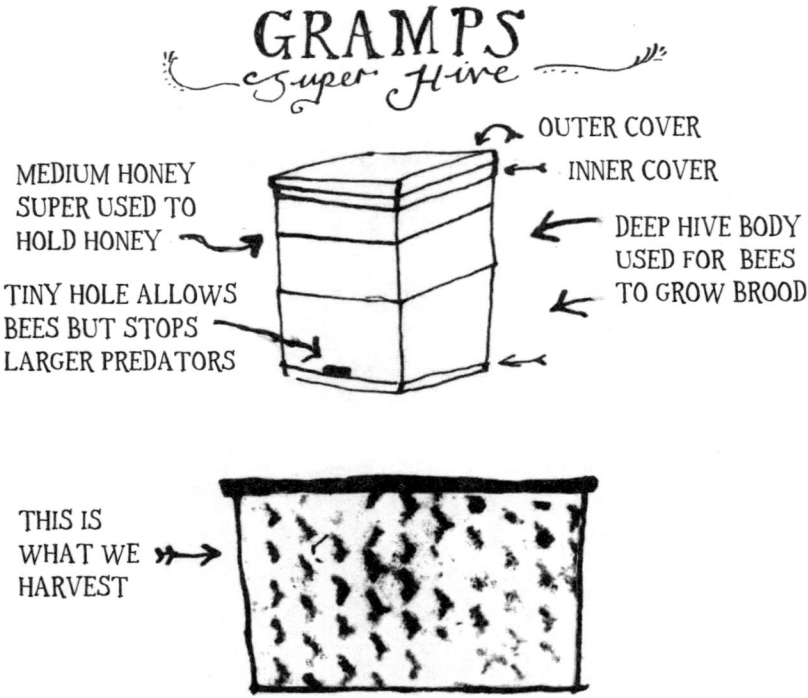

His face was serious again and he didn't need to explain why. There were hardly any bees on the comb and the few that there were didn't seem to know what they were doing.

'What on earth's happened to them all, Gramps?' Ben's voice was shocked.

'No idea. It's a complete mystery. A mystery with a name but no solution.'

Ben's ears pricked up. Could this be the mystery of his own he was so keen to find? Up till now, without any crimes to investigate, he'd only got as far as giving his detective agency a name – Benjamin Busby, Crime Buster. A catchy name was important he thought. But now – well, this could be just the investigation he needed to launch it.

I've got to get to the bottom of this, he thought. *If I can, I won't only be helping Gramps to save the bees – I'll make my reputation as a detective at the same time.*

Just a minute! Hadn't Gramps said that this was a world-wide problem? OK. Roll over, Lulu and Lee, Leading Lady Detectives. An internationally famous super-sleuth that's what I'm going to be!

Suddenly Grandpa's last words came back to him – 'a mystery with a name but no solution'.

He looked at Gramps. 'So what is the name of the mystery?'

'Colony Collapse Disorder – but that's just a fancy way of saying that bee colonies are vanishing and no-one knows what to do.'

Colony Collapse Disorder, repeated Ben to himself. The words were somehow familiar.

Chapter Three

 'So what shall we have for supper, Ben?' asked Gramps.

'Chips?' One of the attractions of staying with Gramps was that he was a champion chip-maker. No frozen ones for him.

'And with them?'

'Just ketchup.'

Gramps gave Ben a don't-push-your-luck look. 'I meant do you want peas, beans or broccoli?'

'Beans please.' That gave him an idea. ' Now, Gramps, I was just thinking. You know you're so keen on healthy eating? Well, can I have some of the royal jelly ❁ that's supposed to be so good for you? How about a spoonful or two with some of that creamed rice pudding I love?' He'd spotted a tin in the larder.

Ha – now I've really put Gramps on the spot, he thought to himself. His grandfather had shelves practically dipping under the weight of honey – jars and jars of it, and boxes of honeycomb too. But what intrigued Ben were the little pots of royal jelly he was never allowed to try.

Gramps's reply to his challenge was rapid and irritable.

'How many more times do I have to tell you, Ben? Those tiny jars sell for much more than my honey. In any case, you won't like it and I don't want to waste it. Now how about getting the chip cutter out and I'll get the potatoes.'

'Okay, okay. Keep your eyebrows on,' said Ben, burrowing happily into the cupboard.

Gramps's kitchen was a treasure trove of gadgets – ones that sliced eggs, stoned cherries or turned mashed potatoes into worm shapes – but, without a doubt, the best gadget was his Unique High Performance Automatic Chip Cutter. No competition. One firm jerk on the handle and a large potato was immediately transformed into chunky chips.

As Ben brought the cutter over to the table, his eyes fell again on the paper Gramps had been reading at breakfast. It was called *New Scientist*. Now he understood the meaning of the words he had glimpsed earlier. The headline read: *The Continuing Mystery of Colony Collapse Disorder*. So that was what Gramps had been concentrating on so intently!

Ben realised that solving this mystery wasn't going to be at all easy. Firstly, it was one that baffled not only beekeepers, but even scientists. Secondly, the mysteries that Lulu and her Chinese friend Lee solved usually involved a crime and this didn't seem to be the case here.

Ben thought of the list he'd made of things to do when investigating a crime. One of the ways to find clues, he remembered, was to ask a lot of questions.

Grandpa was already back at the sink, peeling the potatoes. While he waited for him to finish so he could get going with the chip-cutter, Ben tried hard to remember the conversations he'd had with him about the bees' health.

'Gramps,' he began, 'didn't you once tell me that those little parasite things called varroa are getting more common? They eat the bees' eggs, don't they? So if masses more of them are all eating the eggs – that would explain why the bees are vanishing, wouldn't it?'

'Clever idea, Ben, and you're dead right – they're an absolute menace. But it's not the eggs they eat. First of all, they have a cunning way of getting into the hive. They hitch a ride on a bee's back and, once inside, they lay their own eggs in the cells where the queen has laid hers. Then when the little varroa hatch out they start feeding on the developing bees – the bee larvae.'

'You don't mean they actually eat them?' Ben exclaimed. 'Yuck! How horrible!'

'They're too small to eat them entirely. But they cause terrible damage to the larvae. The poor things develop into bees with horrible deformities and stunted little wings and so they're as good as dead. They don't last long.'

'Gross!' Ben was silent for a moment, half fascinated, half repelled at the idea of the deformed bees.

Well, varroa couldn't be the only culprit, then. Maybe the best thing would be to just encourage Gramps to keep on talking. As he picked up a potato to put into the chip cutter he remembered Farmer Fart.

'Gramps, even if you haven't found lots of bee bodies, and Farmer Bart is careful now, do you think that pesticides are still part of the problem?'

There was an angry snort from Grandpa.

'Do I think they're part of the problem?' He snorted again even louder. 'You see, Ben, if they're designed to kill pests, then they're obviously dangerous for all insects. And now there are even more dangerous new kinds, which have been temporarily banned in some countries.

But, I'll tell you what, Ben,' he added enthusiastically, 'there's a demonstration in London while you're here. BAN DANGEROUS PESTICIDES – *FOREVER!* We could go up by train.'

'Yeah. Right. That does sound like fun,' said Ben without enthusiasm. He knew that demonstrations usually involved a lot of walking.

Gramps's face lost its eager look, but he carried on. 'You haven't forgotten about Action Man, have you?'

Oh no, here we go, thought Ben, but all he said was, 'Yes, you told me about him first when I got my *Spider-Man* costume.' He certainly remembered how he'd loved capering about in that shiny, massive-shouldered outfit.

'So maybe you'll remember what I said then – that you don't have to have superpowers to fight evil?' Gramps continued. 'Anyone can do it if they take action in support of the things they believe in.' He paused. 'People mostly don't, though. And that's how evil triumphs,' he finished flatly.

Ben thought about that for a minute. 'In comics it's the goodies who win actually. They use their superpowers and they defeat the baddies. Films too, Gramps. Think of James Bond.'

'Exactly. Like you say, in comics and films,' said Gramps darkly. 'Unfortunately people don't have superpower vehicles and gimmicky gadgets in real life. All they can do is unite and fight for what they believe in and then, just sometimes, they do defeat the baddies. And that's the way to be an Action Man.'

But Ben didn't want to be distracted by Gramps's ideas about Action Man. He was much more excited by his mention of 'how Evil Triumphs'.

Defeat the Baddies. How exciting that sounded. But what was an Action Man, exactly? The way Gramps explained it, it sounded almost as if Action Men and Triumphing Evil were real beings. Beings about which Gramps obviously knew something . . .

A most appetizing smell of chips was coming from the deep fryer. Ben's mouth was watering as he got the ketchup out. They'd planned to watch a DVD while they had supper. Best to carry on questioning Gramps first thing tomorrow morning.

They piled their meal on to plates and, with trays on their knees, sat on the sofa watching *The Empire Strikes Back*. Much as Ben loved the film, before the end he was having a bit of difficulty keeping his eyes open. Then he looked at Gramps and saw that his eyes were fully shut while his mouth was open and drooping.

'Wakey, wakey, Grandpa,' he said. 'Time for bed.'

Chapter Four

Ben loved climbing up the narrow staircase that led from the upstairs landing to his own private space. He realised other people might find his room inconvenient – tall people especially. Because it was in the attic, the ceiling sloped steeply and there wasn't much space to stand upright. But the massive roughly carved beams supporting the roof made you feel that you had the ribs of some ancient, upturned wooden boat over your head.

He always had fantastic dreams when he slept there. Once he'd found himself in a sailing ship that could fly through the air as well as sail over the water. But tonight the magic wasn't working. In fact, he was having difficulty in sleeping at all. He couldn't get the empty hives out of his head. Then Gramps's face with a long, sad expression floated into his mind. It was the same long, sad expression that his face had been slumping into in the last couple of days every time he thought his grandson wasn't looking.

Ben felt a bit guilty now that he hadn't agreed to go on the march. He hastily switched his mind back to the royal jelly.

Why was Grandpa so sure he wouldn't like it? Obviously he'd forgotten that Ben ate all kinds of exotic things that children weren't supposed to like – salty olives, pickled onions and strong, smelly cheeses. So how to get his hands on the royal jelly without his grandfather noticing? He'd tell him afterwards how much he liked it!

Then he remembered how Gramps had fallen asleep in front of the TV. All this stress about the bees had obviously made him very tired. When he got to bed, he was bound to sleep soundly till the morning. Ideal opportunity!

But there was still light showing under his door. What on earth was Gramps still doing? They'd come upstairs to bed together.

Hurry up, Gramps, he thought drowsily. *I'll have gone to sleep if you don't get a move on.*

But soon – or was it much later? Ben wasn't sure which – he opened his eyes and saw the light was gone and the house was completely quiet. Gramps must have got into bed without him hearing. Now was his opportunity.

He was out of bed and down his private staircase in seconds. But, as he started tiptoeing along the landing to the main stairs, there was a massive creak. Jeez, he'd forgotten how flipping noisy the old floorboards were.

He tried to tread more lightly, but as he approached Gramps's door there was an even louder protest from the floorboards. He froze, not even daring to breath, waiting for a sound from his grandfather's room. Nothing but the occasional snore. Sound asleep. Ben smiled to himself. *Now if I can just make it to the stairs.* He started creeping along again.

Ben heaved a great sigh of relief when he reached the kitchen and had shut the door quietly behind him.

Right. Should be straightforward now.

Everything looked shadowy and mysterious in the dark. Even with the splash of moonlight coming in through the window Ben couldn't make out where Gramps's stores were.

*Right, some ligh*t, he thought as he felt for the switch. Immediately the kitchen was its familiar self. Ben went over to the shelves. Higgledy piggledy as the rest of Gramps's house was, his honey and his other bee products were lined up as orderly as ranks of soldiers. A few minutes later Ben had one of the coveted pots in his hand.

How precious it looked with its shiny top and gold label: BUSBY'S PUREST ROYAL JELLY.

I'll open it, he thought, *just to see what it looks like.* Carefully he twisted the lid, only to find that a gold foil seal covered the contents. Blast, once he'd taken that off there was really no chance of Grandpa not finding out that the jar had been opened. Oh well. He went to the cutlery drawer to get a spoon.

Carefully Ben peeled off the foil and plunged in the spoon. He had imagined a sort of golden jelly tasting of apricots or peaches and was disappointed to find that it was pale and milky and rather sour-tasting.

Royal jelly is supposed to make you feel strong and healthy, isn't it? he thought to himself. But the truth was that his legs had suddenly got jelly-like themselves and, oh no, his hand seemed to be losing its grip on the spoon. And, a second later, it had clattered to the floor.

As he bent to pick it up, the royal jelly slipped out of his other hand and landed with a loud crash on the stone floor. Before he had time to worry about what he'd say to Gramps about the smashed jar he caught sight of something terrifying protruding from his pyjama sleeve.

He'd been stretching his hand out towards the spoon, but now where his hand should have been was something thin and black flailing around helplessly. As he trembled, it did too. For his arm was no longer an arm. It had become the leg of an insect. And his hand? Where was his hand? He tried pulling his fingers and thumb together as if to grasp the spoon and saw the funny little hooky thing at the end of the insect leg make a pinching movement.

Ben hardly had time to take in the full horror of this transformation when he was distracted by a nasty prickly sensation as though something was trying to burst through his skin. It felt as if hairs were sprouting out all over his body. After the prickliness came a horrible pinching sensation as if his body was a piece of bread dough being roughly twisted and squished. Inside his kneaded, pummelled body, he felt his heart pounding in fear.

But, terrifying as these changes were, there was worse to come. As he straightened up, he found he was no longer his normal height. He couldn't even see the top of the table. In fact, he was underneath it and the table appeared to be growing larger until it towered above him. So he had shrunk too – and was shrinking still.

'Oh no,' he whispered to himself, 'will this ever stop or is this the end of me?'

For a minute or two his dwindling size and sudden hairiness had distracted Ben from all the other changes that were happening to his body. Now he fell forward suddenly to find himself on the ground on six flimsy black legs. Worse, where his own two human legs should have been, there swelled the abdomen of a bee, striped black and orange and covered in golden hairs.

He had actually become a bee!

Ben looked desperately at the huge expanse of floor, at the mountain of glimmering, broken glass and the lake of milky liquid surrounding it. His stomach was still feeling twisted, but this time it was panic causing it.

Stop it! Stop it! OK, I'm a bee, but I'm still alive, aren't I? And Ben carried on trying to bolster his courage. *Why should I be scared anyway? I've always loved stories with magical transformations, haven't I? Well, now it's my turn. I'm in a magic adventure!*

But somehow he didn't feel excited. He couldn't help feeling that it would have better if he'd changed into something larger or more powerful.

Now if I'd become an elephant or an eagle I'd be really eager to test out my new strength. But shrinking into something much smaller than you makes you feel . . . Ben thought about what he felt for a moment . . . *makes you feel incredibly vulnerable.*

And something else they don't tell you in books, Ben thought. *Before you start seeing what adventures are possible with your new body – well, you'd just like to know the way to change back to being yourself.*

And, to add to the problem, there was the problem of a bee's lifespan.

Cats, he knew, could, if they were lucky, live to sixteen. For gerbils it was more like two. Two years wasn't long as a lifespan, but you'd still probably have time to find the way to change back.

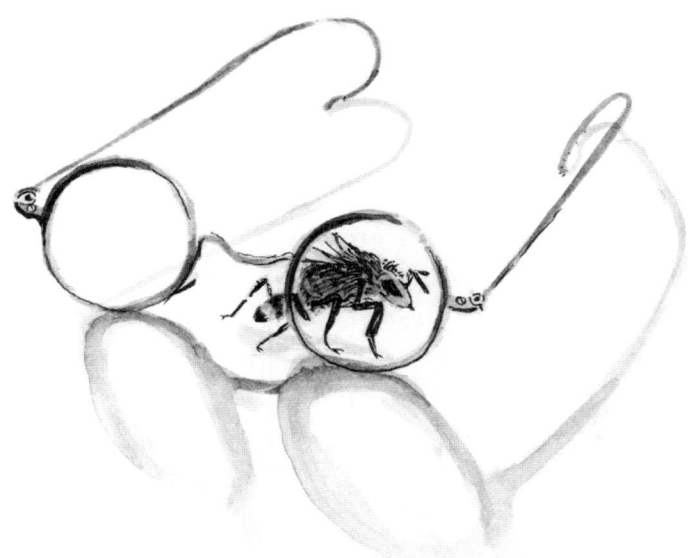

But bees — that was another matter. He needed to remember how long bees lived, but he was pretty sure it was just a matter of weeks or, at best, months. Certainly not years.

'Oh, stop it Ben,' he told himself firmly. 'You're just trying to make yourself panic now. Pull yourself together. Think positively. THINK!'

Maybe there was an antidote to the royal jelly? He knew there was often one for poisons. Now what about that other bee superfood, pollen bread. ● Gramps had tiny jars of it sitting on the same shelf as the royal jelly. Hey, that was probably it. A spoonful or two and it would all reverse — he'd swell and grow, lose these hairs and change back into a boy!

He'd need to check with Gramps, though…to ask Gramps…

How on earth was he going to do that?

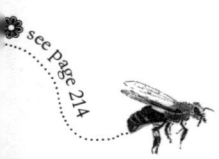
see page 214

Chapter Five

 Ben groaned. Well, he'd meant to, but no sound had emerged. He tried again – and again no sound. Jeepers, if he couldn't groan, how was he going to speak?

'Er, Gramps,' he tried, 'this is me.' Nothing. He tried again. 'It's me, Gramps.' He stopped – stopped trying, that is. In spite of all his efforts, only the faintest, strangest sort of piping sound had come out of his mouth. Well, that was it, then. He couldn't speak to Gramps – or to any other human being either.

Ben was usually a positive and resourceful boy. But he'd never been in a situation where he had so many problems to deal with! The first one was that, even if pollen bread was really the thing that would turn him back to a boy when he wanted, how on earth was he going to lay his hands on some? Hands? He looked helplessly at his little black pincers.

Think laterally – that was Mum's suggestion for when it felt like you were in an impossible situation. Come on. There must be some advantages to being a bee. Think of them. Well, wings, of course. Ben couldn't see if he had any, but he must have, mustn't he? He had all the other features of a bee. And hadn't he always dreamed of flying?

OK. No need to envy Superman now. He could be Buzzy Beeman! Come to think of it, he could be Buzzy Beeman, special investigator. He'd wanted to be the one to solve the mystery of the vanishing bees. This could turn out to be his best chance!

The thing was, could he use his wings? How did they work? The idea of taking off into the air without knowing if he could control them made him a bit apprehensive.

Maybe the first thing would be to try walking on his six legs. **Weird!** But luckily, in becoming a bee, he seemed to have an instinctive ability to coordinate them all. He wasn't racing along six times as fast as usual, though. But then he was a bee not a spider! For speed he had his wings.

Now if I really was a bee, Ben thought, *I'd just fly wouldn't I? I wouldn't sit here thinking, Now I must spread my wings. Now I must lift them up and down. I'd just do it all instinctively like blinking. And what have I got to lose? I'm on the floor anyway so . . . here goes.*

Whee! He was actually lifting off the ground and it felt wonderful and perfectly natural. So, higher and higher above the table and chairs he climbed, up to the shelves now and still climbing. How funny to be level with the kitchen tools hanging on the wall. And how strange they looked now they'd become so enormous. Gosh, that great, shiny metal dome thing was actually the soup ladle!

Wow, hang on. If he kept going up at this rate, he'd hit the ceiling and stun himself. He needed to go forward. Yes, he could do that too. Round and round the kitchen he went now, thrilled with his new ability.

For a while, whizzing and whirling about, Ben lost all his anxiety. But after several minutes more of wheeling and diving giddily he could no longer suppress the little voice inside him that was whispering, 'This is all very good fun, but remember you're on a mission. Don't waste all your energy here.'

Dead right! Gramps's jars of pollen bread were now no use to him at all. If he wanted to try some pollen bread he'd need to get into a hive. He'd watched bees gathering pollen into the little pollen sacs on their legs. Sometimes they looked so laden with the golden grains of pollen they'd gathered that he was surprised they were able to take off again. Now, he needed to find out how they converted it into pollen bread.

And once I get into a hive, he thought, I'm bound to find some clues about what's making the bees disappear.

He realised that while he'd been circling the kitchen the darkness had given way to early morning light. He needed to find a way out of the house. But how? The door to the garden was shut at night and he knew he shouldn't just head towards the nearest window. Once he'd seen a sparrow, which had got into Gramps's kitchen by mistake, nearly stun itself smashing into the glass before they'd opened the door so it could escape.

His best hope was the little window in the larder that Gramps usually left partly open.

Ben didn't feel sufficiently in control of his flying to aim straight for the window and attempt to leave the house in one swoop. Even real insects had trouble flying out through windows. But he had the advantage of understanding about glass. What he could do was approach it slowly, land on the window pane, crawl round the edge of the window and out on to the window sill. Once there he'd be able take flight again.

Chapter Six

 It was a relief to find himself outside on the sill exactly as planned. Now to try his wings and find a hive. He continued to sit there motionless, though.

What was stopping him zooming off? Here he was, a special investigator, with this fantastic chance to explore the life of a bee as a bee himself. And, not only that, he might be able to solve the mystery of bee disappearances from the inside. Why wasn't he fizzing with excitement about setting off on this adventure?

He realised that some words of Gramps were replaying in the back of his mind. They hadn't been scary at the time. Just the sort of interesting stuff about bees his grandfather often told him. Now they were frightening.

'Oh yes, a colony of bees in a hive may have a reputation for being very friendly and cooperative with each other,' he'd said in a grave voice. 'But, make no mistake about it, there's no mercy for anyone they suspect of wanting to steal their honey. They turn upon intruders and attack them viciously. Robber bees, and

there are a few of those around, you know, Ben, usually end up dead.'

No! Don't start thinking like that, he told himself as he started to shiver. Wasn't there something else Gramps had added about the robber bees? Think, think! Then he remembered. Not to appear frightened – that was the trick of it.

Gramps had gone on to explain how bees quickly notice a timid, cowering intruder trying to get into the hive without attracting attention, and launch an attack immediately. But an experienced hive robber, brazen and bold, would sometimes manage to slip past the guards unnoticed. ❁

'Brazen and bold, that's the way,' Ben muttered to himself. Once he got going he'd stop worrying, wouldn't he?

And as soon as he lifted his wings and took off he did feel better. It was thrilling to beat his wings rapidly and feel himself ascending. Wow, this was awesome – rising and rising towards the blue sky.

He was actually way above the trees now. Seen from above they looked like large pieces of broccoli. As he rose further, Gramps's smallholding became a toy farm with tiny chickens, ducks and geese. The orchard and vegetable garden, the field with the beehives had all shrunk. Hey steady on, he warned himself. Carry on like this and I'll be into completely unknown territory in a couple of minutes. Don't want to get lost.

Best to drop height and explore Gramps's garden with his new bee's-eye view. But he found it difficult to recognise where exactly he was. This was partly because he was swooping over bushes and skimming over hedges and not following the paths he used when he was on foot. The other problem was that he couldn't see very well.

No, that wasn't true. He was seeing extremely well, only differently. It was as if a filter had been put over his eyes and the world had changed colour.

Now what was that expression Mum sometimes used about people who always have a very optimistic and kindly view of things? Got it. Mrs Whatever-her-name-was always sees the world through rose-tinted glasses. Well, it was exactly as if he was seeing the world through blue-tinted glasses.

Gramps's garden had become a strange, exciting paradise of intense colours as the blues and blue-purples of buddleia bushes, clumps of nepeta and lavender, and groups of alliums and scabious all competed for his attention. It was as if the flowers were exerting a strange magnetic power on him.

He flew lower and found himself drawn to some unfamiliar flowers whose blossoms were covered with bees. Then he saw something that he recognised immediately – a clump of green spears a bit like grass but taller.

Chives, he realised. So he was in Gramps's herb garden.

And the flowers attracting all those bees must be marjoram and borage. Gramps had told him that they were two of the bees' favourite flowers.

'Grow them more for their benefit than for cooking. I should look up what to use them with,' he'd said.

As Ben landed on some marjoram blossom among the foraging bees, a plan flashed into his head. It was very likely that these were some of Gramps's surviving bees and, if he was lucky, in a minute, they would set off back to their hive. He just had to follow them!

He watched and waited patiently as they darted from flower to flower. Suddenly one took off into the air with another right behind. Right, this was it. He was after them.

They made straight for the meadow, Ben in pursuit, and there were the sloping roofs of Gramps's hives below them. The two bees swooped down towards one of them. Ben felt an unpleasant cramping sensation in his abdomen. Was it fear of his ability to land as they had on the little board in front of the hive? Or fear that, even if he did manage, he would immediately attract the attention of the guard.

'Brazen and bold,' he muttered to himself as he, too, came to land.

Better still, the entrance was surrounded by clouds of bees arriving and departing. What luck! It was one of the few healthy hives.

I'll never be noticed in this buzzing throng, he reassured himself. *Oh yes, with a bit of luck, I'll be able to enter the hive without attracting the attention of the guards. OK. Here goes. Brazen and bold.*

He swooped down towards it.

He wasn't feeling at all bold, actually, for he knew the real danger still lay ahead of him.

Luckily, there were a lot of other bees on the landing board.

Should be able to get inside without attracting any attention.

But he was challenged immediately by a brisk voice coming from a bee right next to him.

'Hustle along,
Bustle along,
Set off in haste,
No time to waste,' it said.

What on earth did that mean? It was clearly a warning of some kind. Luckily, though, it wasn't the one he'd feared: 'Thieving bee, prepare to die!'

Ben quickly looked round to see where the voice was coming from. A bee somewhat bigger than him was staring at him intently with her large, black eyes.

Ben started to tremble. *This is it*, he thought, *I've been rumbled. She's telling me to go before I'm attacked.* He tried to lift his wings and take flight. Nothing happened. Not so much as a twitch. His legs, then. Again, nothing. His bee skills were lost. He was frozen to the spot.

The bee was still watching him intently. But when she spoke again her voice had become more gentle.

'Don't look so scared, little bee.
Just out of the nursery
That's plain to see.'

Ben's stiff body relaxed a little. Clearly the bee was not suspicious of him. He couldn't help feeling offended by her words, though. Little bee? Nursery? What on earth did she take him for?

Suddenly he remembered the timetable he'd made with Gramps a couple of years ago. On a wet day he'd used one of Gramps's reference books to list all the different things bees do in their short lives. He remembered that 'the nursery' meant the

brood cells where the youngest worker bees looked after and fed the little larvae. ✿

Great! If she'd taken him for a little worker ✿ out on its first day of foraging, that meant he'd been accepted and she wouldn't be suspicious that he didn't have much of an idea of what he was supposed to be doing.

Without waiting for his reply, the bee now issued another order,

'Follow me, follow me.
There's all the world for you to see.'

He decided to obey her and he launched himself into the air behind her.

But, though he kept fairly closely on her tail, he just couldn't resist the occasional swoop up into the air above her, or a dive down below her. She didn't seem to be minding his aerobatics so, **Whee!**, he decided to try a little loop-the-loop too and began to curl around in the air as he'd seen pilots doing in air shows. Immediately his dizzy circling was interrupted by the rhyming bee's curt voice.

'Cease your antics
And follow me!
Do just what I say
And take care not stray.

Many workers are lost,
And at what a cost!
Because bees too young to fly
Now sicken and die.'

Ben swiftly finished his loop to end up right behind her. Better not risk annoying her. By her side he should get into the hive safely. Just as important, she seemed to know why the bees were disappearing.

Her rhyme was puzzling, though. What did she mean by 'at what a cost'? And why were the young bees dying? Yes, he certainly needed to stay with her and discover more!

He followed her as she flew down to some wildflowers in the meadow below. As she perched on a foxglove, she addressed Ben again, more gently this time:

'The sun is up,
The air is warm,
From the heart of the flower
There's nectar to be drawn.'

She disappeared straight into the flower, apparently assuming that Ben would know what to do. Well, he was just going to have to take the plunge.

If all goes well, he thought, *while I'm inside the flower sucking the nectar, the pollen in the flower will be sticking to the hairs on my body.*

He'd completely convinced himself that pollen bread, or maybe even the pollen alone, would be the solution to his predicament. But would he need to take it back to the hive in his pollen sacs ❁ and find out how to convert it to pollen bread? Or would the pollen brushing over his body like specks of gold act like fairy dust and turn him back into a boy?

What if he suddenly became a bee-sized boy and got trapped inside the flower? Or perhaps his transformation would be accompanied by a sudden explosion of growth so that –

whoosh! – he blew up to his full size as quickly as he'd shrunk to the size of a bee. So then would he explode out of the flower backwards like a boy-rocket in reverse and land – splat! –in the middle of a bush?

But he was wasting time perched on the outside of the flower. "Bustlealong", as Ben had privately named her, would be out of her flower any second to see how he was getting on and might take him for a lazy bee. He felt his antennae twitching with delight at the powerful scent of the nectar, but how was he going to find the nectar?

He looked at the flower and noticed that it had colour markings that he'd never seen before. Were they only visible to bees' eyes? It was as if the flower was a sort of landing strip and the marks were arrows guiding him in. He followed them deep into the flower and, before he knew it, his tongue had shot out and was sucking away.

The only problem was that he wasn't tasting it at all. His bee tongue was like a long drinking straw and the nectar was being pumped straight into his nectar tank. Never mind. He just needed to fill it up and get back to the hive. Once there he'd surely get some honey for breakfast. He was certainly feeling hungry now.

He emerged from the flower, powdered with golden pollen, but nothing else had changed.

Just as well, he told himself. *I haven't been inside the hive yet and I'd be much better off trying the pollen bread when I've had a chance to do some investigating.*

He looked around for Bustlealong. She was bottom up in a nearby flower, and had reversed out and pushed herself into another almost before Ben could properly see her. It seemed he was going to have to keep going for a while to fill his nectar tank before they went back to the hive. Several flowers later it was relief to hear,

'Don't be slow!

Back we go.'

No time for chatting, then. When was he going to get a chance to ask Bustlealong to explain her puzzling rhyme about the lost bees?

They both winged back to the hive, but this time, with Bustlealong at his side, Ben felt excitement bubbling up as he approached the entrance. In just a moment he would become **Ben Busby – the First Human Ever to Enter the Secret Kingdom of the Bees.**

Chapter Seven

'You twit,' said Ben to himself as he scrambled through the hole after Bustlealong, only to find himself in total darkness. 'Thought they had electricity, did you?' He was straining to see anything at all in the dense blackness, never mind what the bees were up to. The only source of light was the entrance hole.

But hang on! If his eyes weren't giving him much information, his other senses were. He could feel the movement of the bees around him. And the air was not only full of the busy whirring of a multitude of wings but had a dense sweetness that made it delicious to inhale.

Wow, this smells better than a sweet shop, he thought.

As he paused for a moment, enjoying the honey-scented air, a bee about his own size suddenly poked out her tongue at him. Ben stared at her.

'Come on,' she said bossily, 'out with yours.'

Whatever could she want? Was this some kind of greeting? But there was nothing friendly in her tone.

He looked questioningly at Bustlealong and saw that she, too, had been approached by a bee with her tongue protruding and she had immediately stuck out her own. Their two tongues united in a kind of tongue lock. Ew! Gross! However was he going to get out of this?

But the bossy bee nudged him and said brusquely 'Hurry up. Think I've got all day to stand here with my tongue out, do you?' This attracted Bustlealong's attention. She had now separated herself from the other bee.

'You'll concentrate the nectar
When you pass it to and fro,
Adding special vitamins
To help the larva grow.'

So that was the reason the bees locked tongues. Neat really – once you understood. Still, the idea of actually doing it himself gave him exactly the same sick feeling he got when he saw warm milk with skin on the top. Just the idea of swallowing milk with horrible bits of skin in it made him want to throw up. Whatever was he going to do?

But Bustlealong's watchful eye was on him. There was no escape. OK. Maybe now he was a bee it wouldn't feel as disgusting as it looked. He reluctantly extended his tongue. The bossy bee immediately attached hers and started sucking. Actually, it didn't feel disgusting at all. A bit like sucking through a straw but in reverse. In a few seconds the contents of his nectar sac were gone. And he still hadn't got to taste it!

Ben looked round. Bustlealong was now swaying herself from side to side in a strange manner. She immediately attracted the attention of two other bees, who rushed over looking as if they were about to bite her. Apparently unworried, she called to Ben,

'Shake and wiggle,
Wiggle and shake,
There's plenty of pollen
For all to take.'

A moment later Ben felt three eager mouths pecking at his legs. Ben's stomach was now growling fiercely with hunger. 'You'd have thought it would be us, the hardworking foragers who'd be offered some breakfast. But, oh, no, it's me they're treating as a flipping meal-deal special!' he grumbled to himself.

Bustlealong started fidgeting. She'd obviously become impatient with the two bees who were so enjoying the grains clinging to her body. She shook them away and started to store away her pollen load.

'Empty your pollen sacs into a cell,
Push down the grains to pack them in well,' she instructed Ben.

He tried to imitate her, but it was not all that easy to brush the contents of his sac into a cell. He looked around him and saw that there was just as much pollen around the cell as in it.

'Leave the scattered pollen
For others to put away.
They'll collect and store it.
We'll be on our way.'

Huh. Too right! I bet they'll be happy to come and collect it and probably half of it will end up in their mouths, he thought. He looked around furtively. *If only Bustlealong would take her eyes off me for one second I could grab a few mouthfuls too.* But, before he'd had a chance to taste any at all, Bustlealong was hurrying him along again:

'Don't be slow!

Back we go.'

'Don't be slow?' said Ben to himself. 'Huh. Like she ever gives me the chance!'

Twice more, to and fro, from hive to flowers and back again, they went. Each time they pumped themselves to the brim with nectar and then returned to deliver their load to a waiting worker. But, if Bustlealong didn't seem too bothered about eating, Ben was wondering if by now he'd not only missed breakfast but lunch too.

Ben often watched bees bobbing about in the lavender in the summer, but he'd never guessed how incredibly hard they were working. Were they all as industrious as Bustlealong or was she a workaholic?

Darting from flower to flower, he started to formulate a plan. Surely all the contact he'd had with the bees in the hive must mean that he now had its own distinctive smell on him? So he'd nothing to fear from the guards any more. And he knew where the pollen was kept. Could he risk helping himself to some maybe? Or was the pollen store he'd seen just for the nurse bees to feed the larva?

Perhaps workers had special times and places to eat. One thing he was sure of – his investigation would progress much better once he'd eaten. You needed a full stomach to reach maximum brain power! His best bet was to follow Bustlealong back once more. But this time when they entered the hive he would hang behind for a minute until he lost her in the teaming masses. Then he'd have a chance to explore the hive properly.

Things didn't go quite as planned, though. By pausing on the threshold, he'd immediately got himself noticed.

Chapter Eight

'Up hurry, up hurry,' a brisk voice cried.

Oh no, here we go again! Ben thought.

He turned round to find not Bustlealong but a bee about his own size. Ben stared at her. He somehow had the impression she was teasing him rather than ordering him around, but he couldn't be sure. She didn't wait for his reply anyway.

'You are Uphurry of friend?' She had her head to one side as if she were asking him a question, but it sounded like gobbledegook. Then Ben caught on and realised she must mean Bustlealong.

'Bustlealong, do you mean?' he asked. Then, to be sure the bee would understand, he imitated Bustlealong's style,

' "No time to stop,

Work till you drop." Do you mean her?'

Ben felt a grin inside him then realised they were now both waggling their antennae at each other in amusement.

'Do I. Do I,' replied his new friend, Frontoback, emphatically.

'Very bossy, isn't she?'

'Well means she.'

'Yes, she is kind,' Ben agreed. 'She's taught me a lot.'

This was the longest conversation Ben had had since becoming a bee and he was enjoying himself. Then it occurred to him that, since Frontoback knew Bustlealong, there was a good chance she'd be able to explain her mysterious rhyme.

'She spoke to me about all the bees who are getting lost,' said Ben.

' "Too many are lost

And at what a cost.

Too young to fly,

Bees sicken and die," she said. I didn't understand what she meant by "at what a cost", though.'

Frontoback's expression changed, and she spoke seriously to Ben, without mixing her words up.

'Well, that's why she's such a slave driver, of course. She's anxious, like all of us, that so many bees are going out foraging and never coming back. Yes, we're worried about the lost ones – well, anyone would be! – but what we're really, really frightened of is being the next to go missing.

Of course Bustlealong being Bustlealong doesn't stop to worry about herself. No, she's off trying to work twice as hard to make up for all the lost bees. Noticed her wings, have you?'

Actually, Ben hadn't, but Frontoback didn't wait for him to speak.

'Frayed to a frazzle, aren't they? And she's not that old. She's just worn out her wings with overwork.'

'And what does her rhyme mean?' Ben asked again.

'I'm just coming to that. She'll be thinking about the young bees that don't go out, all the ones who depend on us foragers to bring them food. Well, there just aren't enough of us to do it now, are there? So what happens to the nurse bees inside the hive? They start getting weak or even dying themselves. So the ones that are left are really struggling to feed the larva. Come over to the brood cells and I'll show you.'

Ben lost no time in following her. The non-stop torrent of information that poured from Frontoback was just what he needed for his investigation.

But keeping up with her wasn't easy. He'd started to get used to the constant hustle and bustle of arriving and departing bees near the hive entrance, but he now found the hustle and bustle continued even as you moved away from it.

It was just like being in the underground in the rush hour – with one big difference.

Humans in the tube may be all crushed together, he thought, *but they still try to avoid touching each other if they can.* But the bees were just walking over each other in a perfectly friendly way. Eeh, what was that strange feeling on his back? Like the tickle of small hands or . . . feet, yet he didn't feel crushed or frightened. It seemed perfectly normal.

It even felt normal to be clambering over other bees himself to keep up with Frontoback. And then suddenly it didn't. Walking over bees had become a bit like walking on a moving walkway because the bees under him were moving too. But suddenly he trod on some bees who didn't move at all. Who felt stiff. Who felt . . . dead. Ben's heart stopped. He scrambled off the dead bees as quickly as he could and looked at them in horror. Frontoback stopped too.

'Oh, come on! Don't tell me that hasn't happened to you yet? I know we never used to find dead bees in the hive, but there are so many around now. The undertaker bees are too hungry and weak to move the bodies out of the hive straight away. Sometimes it takes two or three of them to shift a body.

So there's your answer. Not much of a riddle really, is it? "Workers are lost and at what a cost"? Simply means that when worker bees vanish all the bees in the hive slowly starve.'

Now Ben understood why Bustlealong didn't encourage snacking. If the honey supplies were getting short, they were probably rationed.

'What I don't understand is why all the workers are disappearing,' he said quietly as he followed her.

'Well, that *is* the big mystery, of course. I mean *we* of all insects to be getting lost! Always being told – aren't we? – that we're the greatest navigators in the world. With our special waggle dance ✿ telling other bees where to find nectar and—'

She was interrupted by two hurrying bees who abruptly pushed her forward. Ben felt others doing the same to him.

What on earth is going on? he thought, wishing he could get out of the way. This wasn't the usual casual contact of bee body to body in the crowded hive. He'd been shoved – and not accidentally, either. He was caught up in a powerful forward surge – and the reason for its urgency was soon clear.

'Help, help! Emergency! Reinforce the guards,' bees were

see page 215

calling. The next moment he caught sight of two guards desperately trying to restrain a large wasp that had managed to enter the hive. It was thrashing around wildly as it tried to shake them off. The bee reinforcements wasted no time in joining the attempt to pin the wasp down. Two seized hold of its antennae and immediately started to bite them.

Ben had never had the affection for wasps that he had for bees. So when Frontoback grabbed hold of one of the wasp's legs and called to him to do the same he attempted to imitate her. But the wasp, though now completely outnumbered, was still kicking about furiously and, try as he might, Ben couldn't catch hold of a leg.

Frontoback, however, had transformed into a pitiless warrior, tugging at the leg she'd grasped until she'd pulled off a number of segments. Finally she wrenched the entire leg off.

Another bee was tearing at one of the wasp's wings, which was half pinned beneath its body. That looked easier than trying to catch a leg, so Ben joined her in biting and tearing it apart. The wasp was slowing down now in its wild flailing about. Ben looked up and saw the reason why. A bee was crunching energetically at the narrow point where the wasp's abdomen joined its thorax. It was gruesome, but Ben couldn't tear his eyes away.

So he didn't notice the two bees doing the same thing at the point where the wasp's head was attached to its thorax – till he heard a victorious cry and saw the wasp's head rolling towards him.

Ben gazed at it in horror for a moment, too shocked to move.

Luckily cleaner bees arrived to shift the wasp's dismembered body parts. As two of them began pushing the head towards the hive entrance, Frontoback returned to his side.

'So, do you remember how in awe we were of the forager bees when we were little?' she asked, as if nothing had happened. As usual she didn't wait for an answer. 'How we longed to be allowed to fly off like them to collect nectar? Creeping caterpillars, you can't have forgotten all the training we did when we were first allowed out on flights to be sure we had the navigational skills to get back to the hive safely. And now it's us, the Super Bee, Special Power Foragers, who are getting lost!'

Ben thought quickly. Though this was interesting it still didn't explain why the forager bees were disappearing.

Luckily Frontoback was unstoppable. She'd only paused to take a breath and continued, 'It's all the illnesses that are causing it. Of course, I don't need to tell you that. Bet you're often feeling pretty sick yourself. But for some bees it's much worse. To begin with it was just a few, but now there's masses of them getting this horrible dizziness. Where have you been actually, snailbrain, not to have been seeing bees?' She stopped suddenly. 'Just look over there.'

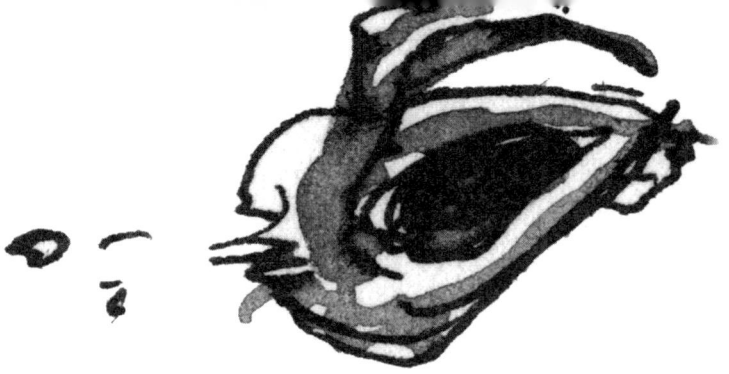

Ben followed her gaze and saw three bees staggering around in a slow, confused way. Then one stopped moving altogether. Not waiting for Frontoback, Ben was at the side of the collapsed bee, trying to help her to get on her feet again. Try as he might to support her, she didn't seem to have any strength in her legs. She was desperately trying to say something to him, but her voice was too feeble for him to hear what it was.

'Wait a second. I'll get my friend. Together we'll—'

But the bee suddenly found some strength and gasped, 'Don't worry about me. I'm . . . done for, but you . . . you beware of the oilseed. She was staring at him intently as if she was trying to say more, but her little voice trailed away. Then she fell on to her back and struggled to speak again

'. . . Oilseed rape,' she managed. Then, in a feeble whisper that Ben could barely hear, 'And . . . k-keep away from the Oppies and Ogwood too. They're all . . . all . . . k-killing us.' Her legs twitched for a moment and then they were still.

Ben felt his own legs wobbling. Frontoback noticed him shaking his head in distress.

'There's nothing we could have done,' she comforted him. Once they start getting dizzy – they're done for. Look at those two. They've got no idea where they're going. Imagine what will happen if they try going out again. Not much chance of them getting back again, is there? Their ability to navigate has been completely messed up.'

'She was trying to warn me. "Beware of the oilseed" . . . I think that's what she said.'

Frontoback just looked at him without answering.

'The Oppies, then. Who are they? She said they'd killed her.'

'I've no idea who she meant. Tell you what, though. It'll have something to do with the Big Ones. Some of them are very dangerous.' Her voice was bitter.

This sounded exciting to Ben. He had no idea what or who the Big Ones were, but they certainly sounded like prime suspects. "The Big Ones . . . ?" he repeated in a puzzled tone, hoping to encourage Frontoback to continue – and it worked.

'You obviously don't know much about them, do you? Probably think they are all like those nice White Ones with hoods who feed us in winter, don't you? Huh. Well, believe me, they're not all like that. As I said, there are some really dangerous types.'

'Dangerous types?' echoed Ben.

'The Invisible Ones are the worst. What they do is persuade the farming kind to use all kinds of poisonous things to kill us.'

'How on earth do they manage that? Farmers need bees for their crops, don't they?'

'Well, *they* think they're just protecting their crops from pests, but when they kill the pests they kill us too, of course.

Yep, "sicken and die" just about sums it up,' she finished gloomily.

'Who are the Invisible Ones?'

'That's the whole point, snail brain. We don't know who they are because they're invisible, but they are out there all right. Oh yes, see them or not, they're out there.'

Chapter Nine

They both fell silent. Ben was thinking hard. It really seemed as if he had just about all the pieces to solve the puzzle. If only he could somehow find out who or what the Invisible Ones were. Might Grandpa . . .

His thoughts were interrupted by a little voice,

'Nothing to do, you two, but sit looking at each other? I was thinking of getting a snack before setting off to work myself,' it piped.

The voice came from a very curious little bee crawling towards them. She seemed to have something the matter with her because her movements were very awkward. Ben realised that not only did she have a bumpy, lumpy shape different to any bee he had ever seen before but her wings were crumpled and stunted.

Frontoback saw him looking at her. 'That's Wonky and she's my mate,' she said. 'Yep, we hang out together.'

Ben could see why you'd want to hang out with Wonky. She was small and a bit misshapen maybe, but she was friendly and she'd come up with the best suggestion he'd heard since he'd joined the hive.

'Hello, Wonky,' he said. 'Pleased to meet you. Did I hear you say snack?'

'Certainly did. If you're interested – follow me.'

'Sounds good,' said Frontoback.

'I'll be right behind you', added Ben. The trouble was that keeping right behind them turned out to be practically impossible. He just wasn't as used to clambering over any bee in his path as they were. He was also worried that if he let them out of his sight for a second he might never find them again. He couldn't be sure of picking out Frontoback in a throng of similar-looking bees and, though Wonky was much more recognisable, she was so small that she would vanish from sight immediately if a pair of bees chose to walk over her.

Hard as he tried to keep them in view, when he approached the side wall of the hive he found that they had disappeared. Simply vanished into thin air. Ben looked at the wall in alarm. He couldn't see another exit. So they must still be inside somewhere. His eyes travelled up the wall and he realised straight away what had happened. While he'd been looking around the bottom of the wall, they'd carried on walking – upwards.

'Twit,' Ben said to himself. He'd watched bees half his life without really registering that they spend quite a lot of their time moving vertically – just like rock climbers. He'd seen films of people rock climbing, though, and it looked slow, difficult and scarily dangerous.

The bees, however, were moving upwards and downwards

just as effortlessly as they moved along the ground. How on earth was he going to follow Frontoback and Wonky now?

'Come on, come on. No time to be hesitating or you'll lose them altogether,' he told himself. 'You found out how easily you could fly. Now try wall walking. You've got six legs after all. Could turn out to be fun.'

Ben started off after Frontoback and Wonky and in seconds found he wasn't even aware that he was climbing at all. He was scuttling upwards as naturally as if he were a lizard. In only a minute or two he had caught up with Frontoback and Wonky – just in time to hear Wonky say, 'Hey, guys, the honey here is just ready for eating. Dip in. Dip in.'

Ben didn't need a second invitation.

He saw Wonky had led them to a part of the comb where the cells were just about to be capped. He knew many wings had fanned the nectar to convert it to honey. Now it was ready to be stored for the winter and bees were busy putting a seal of wax on some of the cells. They took no notice when Ben and his new friends started eating from other cells, which were still open.

'Thimportant to have thomething in your thomach before you thet off to work,' said Wonky thickly through a mouthful of honey.

Ben didn't need any more encouragement. He suddenly realised how famished he was and sucked up the honey greedily. It seemed only seconds later that Wonky looked up, rubbed her front legs over her antennae as if cleaning them, and said, 'Well, that's probably enough now, guys. We'll have to manage on that.' Since Ben wasn't even half full he realised that the

bees were rationing themselves so that their dwindling supplies could feed as many of them as possible.

'Ready for take-off?' asked Wonky cheerily.

Ben had secretly been hoping to hang about in the hive a little longer to see what else he could find out, but Frontoback and Wonky were both so friendly and full of information he couldn't risk losing them. He'd have to follow them.

Wonky set off towards the exit.

Frontoback whispered, 'When we're outside, I like to keep an eye on her.' As they paused on the landing ledge readying themselves for take-off, Ben realised why she was so protective.

There was Wonky wobbling on the edge all ready for take-off, but looking as though the movement of her stunted wings wouldn't carry her anywhere, as though they'd simply slow down her inevitable tumble to the ground.

'So brave, isn't she? You can see why we need to protect her. Most of the wonky ones just fall off the ledge and die. But because her wings are not quite so stunted she can fly short distances. Look at that! She's already taken off! Come on. After her.'

Ben soared off into the air once again, feeling the thrill of being airborne.

It was much more fun going nectar gathering with these two than with the conscientious Bustlealong. Frontoback didn't seem to care about the amount of nectar gathered. Her concern was to make sure Wonky didn't go too far. They darted about the lavender banks close to the hive and Ben found that, in between dips into flowers, there was plenty of time to fool around.

Now this was more like it! Bees had always seemed to him

to be having such fun as he watched them in the lavender, the stems dipping with their weight.

And now he found he, too, could enjoy the sensation as he landed and the slender spear of lavender bent and swayed beneath him. For a moment he was frightened that he would lose his grip and fall but his six legs with their hookey little feet kept him firmly attached and –

Whee! – he soon sprang back up again. This was better than the fair! There, even on the most fearful ride, you were enclosed in a little car of some sort. Now he was in total control!

Suddenly he heard an urgent hiss from FrontoBack,

'Keep still! Stop bobbing about like that.'

Why was she suddenly so annoyed? When Ben turned to look at her, however, he realised she wasn't scolding him for not nectar gathering but warning him of something.

She's petrified, he thought. He followed her eyes upwards and saw the reason for her panic. Hovering above the lavender bush was an enormous and vicious-looking hornet ✿ – three times the size of the wasp.

But Frontoback's warning had come too late. The horrible creature was already watching them with its large black eyes, probably deciding which of them it would dive down and devour first.

'I'm such an idiot,' Frontoback muttered, though

see page 216

whether to herself or to him Ben wasn't sure.

'If only I'd persuaded her to stay in the hive. She'll never get away from him – even if we can.'

'You mean we have a chance to get back to the hive, but she'd be too slow?'

'That's not what I mean at all, dungball! The very last thing we want to do is fly back to the hive. Why do you think he's waiting there? He could easily have flown down and got one of us by now. Then gobbled up the other two for pudding.'

'Seriously?' whispered Ben.

'No, he's hovering there to scare us into trying to escape him by making for the hive. Then he'll follow us back. Oh yes, hornets can be very patient. After all, why hurry when there's a whole hive to eat?'

'He doesn't know where the hive is?' asked Ben.

'Not yet. He plans to watch us go into the hive and then sit patiently on the landing board, waiting for the foragers to return. They're the hornet's favourite – all sweet with nectar.'

'And there's nothing we can do?' asked Ben.

'A mass defence only works with intruders more or less our own size. But with that monster – no chance. Our only hope of saving the colony would have been to lure him away.'

'But l-lure him how?' whispered Ben, trying to control the tremble in his voice.

'We could have set off at top speed in the opposite direction and tried to reach some kind of hiding place before he could catch up with us. But there's no chance of Wonky being able to do that.'

What a desperate plan, thought Ben. *How much chance would we have of keeping ahead of the hornet even if it was just the two of us?*

As for doing it with Wonky – well that was, as Frontoback had realised, impossible.

Their only hope of escape would be to abandon Wonky. Ben immediately felt mean even to have had the thought. Wasn't it better, though, that at least two of them survived?

Suddenly he had a brainwave. They didn't have to abandon Wonky! Only one of them was needed to decoy the hornet. Then the other one could get Wonky back to the hive.

I'm not far from Gramps' house. If I could only reach it and fly inside, I doubt the hornet would dare to follow. So really it should be me that attracts the hornet's attention – and then sets off at top speed, he thought.

To Frontoback he whispered, 'Don't worry. I'll lure it away. You stay here and get Wonky safely back as soon as the hornet chases after me.'

He didn't realise these would be his last words to Frontoback, and didn't wait for her reply. He launched himself into the air before he could have second thoughts. An evil, mechanical whirring sound told him that the hornet was no longer hovering but was now in close pursuit.

Chapter Ten

 Flying was no longer fun. It was now just a desperate effort to keep ahead of the hornet. Ben didn't dare to turn round to see how close it was in case he lost speed, but with that hateful buzzing filling the air there was no doubt that he was horribly near.

Would he be able to keep up this speed until he reached Conkers? And why wasn't Grandpa's house already in sight? His plan to escape the hornet depended on being able to maintain speed just long enough find an open window. If, instead, the hornet caught up with him first, the horrendous insect would devour him in seconds.

Fear and tiredness were making it increasingly difficult for Ben to maintain his very slight lead.

If I don't see the house soon, I'm not going to have enough strength left for a final spurt to get there before the hornet realises what I'm up to, he thought.

He spotted a tree ahead of him. *Right, I'll head for that and see if I can lose the hornet among the branches.* Once screened by the leaves, his smaller size would become an advantage, he reckoned.

As Ben flew nearer to it, his heart flooded with relief. This was not just any old tree, but the chestnut in Grandpa's garden! All he needed to do was head towards the tree and then, having lured the hornet into its green, leafy depths, veer to the right and fly on towards the house. Then he'd disappear through the open window before the hornet had even realised what he was up to. He flew frantically towards the tree and concealed himself amongst its branches.

But the fearful drone of the hornet was still behind him. Maybe he was hidden among the leaves, and wouldn't be seen if he swerved out again towards the house.

'Let the window be open! Let the window be open!' he muttered to himself as he flew.

Yes!

As Ben approached the house, he saw that the little larder window was ajar. He didn't dare slow down, though, and try to land and then get in by crawling through the same way as he'd got out. This time he would just have to trust in the accuracy of his flying and fly through the narrow opening without stopping.

His heart pounding, he hurled himself towards the gap – and found himself back in the kitchen, too weak with tiredness to feel any relief.

He had to hide in case the hornet was still following!

It was a painful effort to keep his wings moving, but, without pausing, Ben flew out into the passage and on and upwards towards his bedroom. The door of his room was open exactly as he'd left it, and in he flew.

Bed! His dear bed. Of course. Under the covers, safely hidden, he could sleep safely. Now it didn't matter that he no longer had the energy to stay airborne. He could simply allow himself to fall – **plump!** – on to his pillow – and he did.

Only to become aware of an insistent whining. No! Not the hornet surely? How could it possibly have followed him into the house? But the ghastly metallic noise was becoming louder. All Ben needed to do now was crawl under the duvet and he'd be hidden. Instead, rigid with fear, he remained unmoving and exposed on the pillow. And then he made another mistake. That menacing noise jarring in his ear like a drill made him want to scream and he heard himself making a very strange sound just at the moment the terrible insect entered the room.

Chapter Eleven

Again, Ben tried desperately to call, 'Help! Help!' but, for all his frantic efforts, he could only make a muffled sound, as if his mouth were full of cotton wool. That little sound had attracted the hornet's attention – but it was no way loud enough to alert a human. Ben shut his eyes in terror as he heard the horrible buzzing approach.

He was the hornet's dinner now for sure. Hornet's Delight, that's what he'd be. Yes, as much of a treat for that greedy monster as Honey Puffs were for him. He was now trembling uncontrollably. A hornet who'd just been tricked out of finding a whole hive would probably find extra delight in tearing him apart before eating him.

'Ben, what's the matter?'

It sounded like his grandfather's voice. No, he was imagining it. But he tried even harder to scream so that Gramps might really hear him.

'Ben, Ben. It's all right, fellow. I'm here. Stop screaming and tell me what's the matter.'

Ben forced himself to open his eyes and saw that his grandfather was really there in the doorway, looking at him very anxiously.

'Quickly, Gramps, save me! That hornet – it's going to eat me!'

'What hornet, Ben?' Gramps looked around as he spoke. 'And they don't eat humans anyway.'

Hadn't Grandpa seen him, then? The room was strangely dark. So perhaps he hadn't yet realised what had happened to him.

'Gramps, look on the pillow. I'm not a human.'

Grandpa came over and sat on his bed.

'Ben, if you're not a human, what are you?'

'I'm a . . .' And then suddenly he felt his grandfather's arms round his shoulders giving him a hug.

'. . . bee,' he finished weakly.

'Ah,' said Grandpa.

'Was,' Ben corrected himself. 'I was a bee. And we'd better be careful because there's a hornet in the room.' But his grandpa smiled reassuringly and patted his arm.

He doesn't believe me, Ben realised.

'All right, I know you think it was a nightmare.' His voice was indignant now. 'But it wasn't!' Gramps continued to look at him quizzically.

Ben noticed his grandfather's expression. 'And don't keep looking at me like that. It was your royal jelly that did it. I only had a spoonful and it happened. I turned into a bee. One spoonful, that's all, and I just sort of shrank and transformed all at once. I was pretty scared I can tell you because I didn't know how I could change back . . .' And the whole story poured out of him.

It took some time for Ben to tell Grandpa everything that happened after his transformation. It was important to him that Gramps knew all about the courage of the bees he'd met and how the colony was struggling to survive. Then he finished with his terrifying flight home, trying to lure the hornet away from Frontoback and Wonky.

'My goodness, that was brave of you. But you can relax now, Ben. You can see there's no hornet here.'

'So you do believe me?'

The lines in Gramps's forehead deepened but he didn't answer.

'Okay, then, come downstairs and I'll show you the jar of royal jelly.' The cat was out of the bag anyway, so he might as well use the shattered jar as evidence of his transformation, he thought, rather than try to clear it up before Gramps had a chance to notice it.

Grandpa followed him. He didn't say, 'So how come you opened the jar when I asked you not to?' Nor did he say, 'Royal jelly doesn't turn boys into bees'. He just waited for Ben to find that there was no fallen jar in the kitchen.

Ben scurried ahead of him. The morning light was still faint so he turned on the kitchen light and looked at the floor. And there it was – the broken jar in a milky pool.

'Now do you believe me?' The furrows on Gramps's forehead reappeared. Ben felt his face flush with indignation as Gramps remained silent.

'And how could I have dreamt all that stuff about the bees, anyway? How would I have known it all if I hadn't actually met them? Come on, Gramps. Tell me how!'

He didn't give his grandfather a chance to reply, though, because he suddenly remembered the most important thing he needed to tell him. 'And you know what else, Gramps,' he carried on excitedly, 'I think I've found part of the answer to why the bees are vanishing. You know – not only dying but disappearing altogether.'

Gramps's mouth fell open. He sat down abruptly and listened silently as Ben continued.

'Frontoback told me stuff about the "illnesses". Mostly it sounded like the things you already know about – like nozema and varroa. Wonky, you remember her? The little misshapen bee I told you about who was so brave? Well, I bet she was partly eaten by a varroa when she was a larva. Anyway, Frontoback said that, on top of all their usual problems, the foragers have a new one. They've been getting so dizzy they can't navigate properly.'

'Dizziness, you say?' Gramps sat forward on his chair. 'Did you see any of the bees who were ill like that?'

Ben swallowed. He didn't like to remember the last moments of that worker bee. He took a deep breath and began.

'Well, that's just it, Gramps. I did try to help one who was already dying. She was gasping horribly but she seemed to want to tell me something. All I could hear, though, was, "Beware of oilseed rape." Such a weird name. I'd no idea what she meant and nor did Frontoback. Then she fell on to her back, dead, before I could ask any more. So, do you have any idea what she was talking about?'

The puzzled lines on Gramps's face had given way to wide-eyed astonishment.

'I think I do, Ben! What you've just told me is amazing! Astonishing! Confirms, you see, what I've been reading about colony collapse disorder. Scientists have been linking the disappearance of the bees with a kind of pesticide that interferes with their nervous system and causes that dizziness you were talking about. Our nervous system takes messages to our brain and it's the same with bees. The pesticides they suspect are called neonicotinoids.'

'That's a mouthful.'

'I'll explain why they're called that. They're a special kind of pesticide used to coat seeds. Then, when the seeds grow into plants, the stuff that kills pests is already there in the plants themselves. The farmers don't have to spray anything.'

'But what's that got to do with their name?'

'Well, these neonicotinoids contain nicotine, you see. It's the stuff that makes cigarettes so dangerous to humans. And it doesn't kill the bees straight away like some other pesticides do. It weakens them and causes them to lose their sense of direction and they get lost.'

He sighed. Ben guessed he was thinking of his own empty hives.

'And those that do get back – well, the pollen they bring back to the hive from treated crops is affected too. It means that all the bees in the colony gradually get weaker. So diseases that bees have always had, but which didn't kill them before, are now fatal. You with me, Ben?'

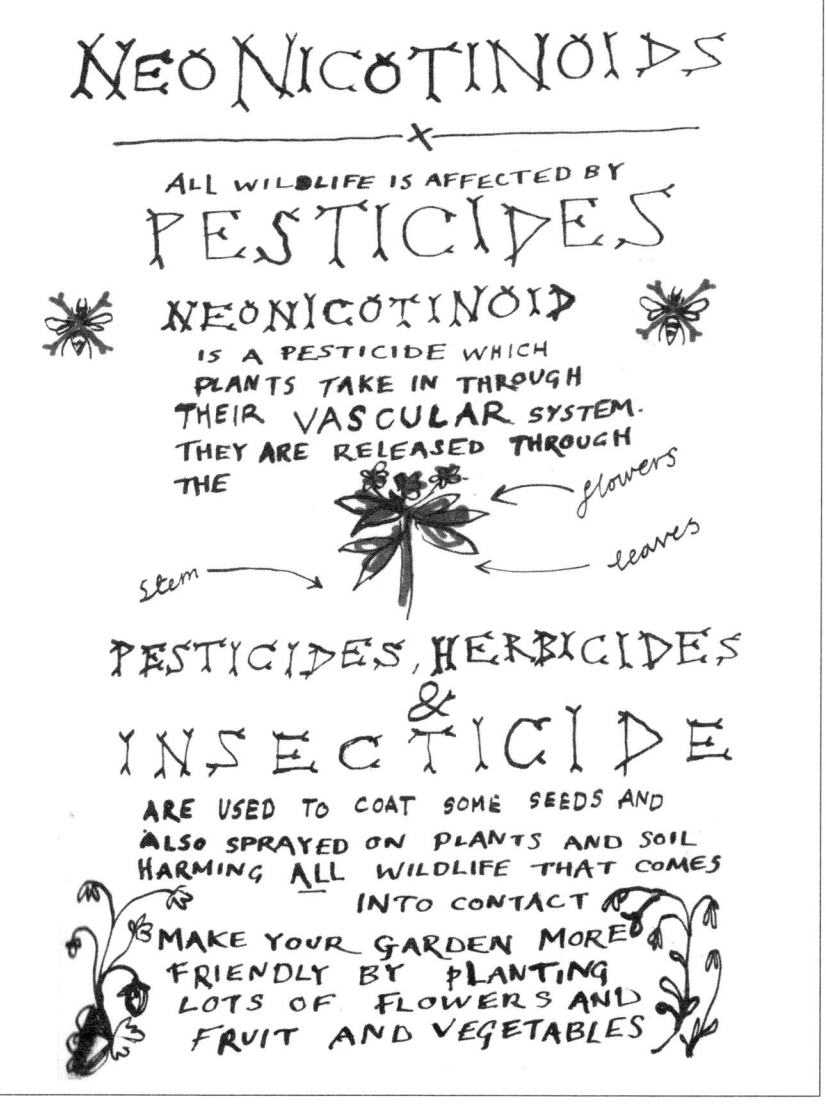

'Course, I am, Gramps. I saw enough dizzy, dying and dead bees myself, I can tell you.'

'Well, now I'm coming to your question about the oilseed rape. You know that bees in a hive go foraging over large

distances, so that they're not all getting nectar from the same flowers or crops? The dying bee will have realised that she started to get sick when she went to a certain crop, oilseed rape, and she seems to have been trying to warn the others to stay away from there. And what she says confirms scientist's suspicions. Oilseed rape is one of the crops most often treated with neonicotinoids, you see.'

Ben jumped up, knocking his chair over as he did so.

'So the scientists have had their suspicions, and what that poor, dying bee said is real evidence!' he exclaimed excitedly. 'And that's not all, Gramps. There's something else Frontoback said. She started talking about "the Big Ones". Well, obviously she meant us humans, but then she said that among them there were some very, very nasty types, and that the worst ones were . . . the Invisible Ones.'

Gramps leaned forward. 'Did she say who they were?'

'I was hoping you might have some idea, Gramps. Frontoback said they encourage the farmers to use poison when they plant crops and I couldn't understand why on earth anyone would want to kill bees. But now it looks like . . .'

'Just a minute, Ben,' Gramps interrupted. 'This is complicated. You get yourself some cereal and I'll try to explain.' Gramps fetched some milk from the fridge and sat down opposite his grandson. Ben had suddenly remembered how starving he was and was pouring a very generous portion of cereal into a bowl. For a moment, the only sound was of Ben crunching honey hoops, then Gramps began to speak. He seemed to be choosing his words carefully.

'Nobody actually intends to kill the bees. But when you think of all the farming that goes on in the world you can see that there's a great deal of money to be made by convincing farmers to use a chemical coating for seeds or some other powerful but dangerous pesticide so that the maximum amount of crops can be grown without being eaten by bugs, or affected by disease.'

'So Frontoback was right,' exclaimed Ben through a mouthful of cereal.

'Yes and no. It's more complex than that. Like I said, no one actually wants to kill the bees but . . . sometimes it's just that people will believe what is convenient for them to believe. So, if there's one pesticide that is particularly successful because it saves the farmers from having to spray the crops – well, you see, it's going to be very hard to convince the farmers and the manufacturers that this particular chemical is having harmful effects, isn't it?'

Ben nodded, still munching. 'So it's the people making the pesticides who are the Invisible Ones. Because the bees know they are dying, but they've never seen the people who've actually provided the poison.' Frowning, he pushed his empty bowl away and sighed deeply. 'Now I really get why you're so keen on going on that demo to persuade the government to ban neonicotinoids. What I can't understand is why the government hasn't done it already.'

'Yes, well.' Gramps's tone was bitter.

'Well what?'

'Well, that needs quite a bit of explanation. Perhaps we should sweep up the glass and think about having some more

to eat before we get into that! I've never seen you finish a bowl of cereal so fast. Get the dustpan and brush will you, Ben? I'll get the mop and bucket.'

Ben's face was serious as he helped clear up, not just because of their conversation but because he felt a strange, sinking feeling. The relief he'd felt escaping the hornet and finding himself back with Gramps had distracted him. Now the sadness at his abrupt parting from his new friends suddenly hit him.

How could he worry about saving bees in general when he didn't know whether Frontoback and Wonky had reached the hive safely? And, even if they had made it back, could the colony survive? He was remembering how tired and hungry the bees had been.

'You know, Gramps,' he said as he put the mop away, 'I've been thinking about the hives which have still got bees. How about we make them some bee toffee like we did that rainy summer, remember, when you thought the bees hadn't been able to get out and find enough nectar?'

Gramps grinned, remembering the sticky mess Ben had created, dividing up the bee fondant into different trays. 'Right, Ben. And perhaps we can even avoid getting stuck to the kitchen floor this time.'

Ben ignored his comment. He was now thinking about the empty hives and remembering what Gramps had said about not wanting to replace them.

'Okay. Second idea. You know you said yesterday that, even if you got some new bees, you wouldn't know how to prevent

them from disappearing again? Well, it's not like you to give up like that. I was thinking . . .' Ben hesitated. 'Well, how about having a word with Chris? I mean, I know he irritates you sometimes, but it could be worth trying some of his ideas.'

Grandpa exploded before he could finish his sentence. 'Don't ask me to speak to that sanctimonious prig again,' he spluttered. 'Had quite enough of him yesterday. "Haven't had so many losses from my hives, Toby, possibly because I make them myself . . . blah, blah, blah. Didn't I suggest to you when I started natural beekeeping that you should try yourself? Think I even suggested I show you how to construct a top bar hive . . . blah, blah, blah." Honestly, talk about smug . . .'

Gramps paused in his indignant imitation of their conversation to take a breath and Ben seized the moment to distract him.

'Come on, Gramps, be fair. Even if Chris is, well, sort of a bit smug, he's not a bad person and he'd always help you, wouldn't he?'

'I'll think about it,' said Gramps non-committally. 'Now, it's about time you had some more breakfast.'

It took only two more substantial bowls of cereal for another brainwave to flash into Ben's mind.

'I've got it, Gramps! We have a Big BuzZ.'

'What would that be, then?'

'I made it up, but, you know, it would be like a school fête, only the activities would be about bees. Competitions for bee costumes, six-legged races, stalls selling bee-friendly seeds – that kind of thing.'

'And this would happen where exactly?'

'Well, your field at the back would be quite big enough.'

'Now, how did I guess? Sounds like a massive amount of work to me.'

'That's the point, isn't it? We'd need help. But the more people we have helping us the more the message about the threats to bees would spread. It might encourage more people to keep bees too.'

Gramps smiled at Ben. 'Well, that makes sense. And it's true there are quite a few people round here who make things they might like to sell. Alison – you know, who supplies the farm shop with her ice cream – does a scrumptious one with acacia honey. Come to think of it, the Woodbines make lovely candles and quite a few other things with their beeswax. I bet they'd be glad to have a stall. And Chris does a wicked honey cake.'

He noticed Ben grinning.

'Okay, Ben. It's true. Chris is a decent bloke. Just didn't choose the best moment for going on about how brilliant natural beekeeping is and what happy, healthy little bees he's got. Anyway, I hope you haven't forgotten that, if we do go around to Chris's, Aurora will be there?'

Ben realised Gramps was having a little dig about a conversation they'd had the day before. In the car on the way home from collecting him from the station, Gramps had suggested to him that, as Chris had his niece, Aurora, who was the same age staying with him, they might all meet up. Aurora! What kind of a name was that?

'Doesn't really sound like my type, Gramps,' he'd said.

'Ben, you're being ridiculous. How can you possibly know that? I haven't said a word about her.'

'It's the name. Don't you think she sounds a bit of a pink glittery type?'

'A what?'

'You know, Gramps – all into make-up and painting her nails sparkly and that kind of stuff.'

A loud snort had emerged from Gramps. 'Honestly, Ben, I've heard of sexism and ageism but you've invented a new prejudice.'

'Which, then? Pinkism or sparklyism?'

'Neither, Ben. I was thinking of nameism. I don't suppose the girl chose her name anyway.'

Luckily, as Gramps had then pulled up in front of the house and got out of the car, he'd dropped the subject – until now.

Groan.

Chapter Twelve

Chris lived only ten minutes away in the car, but as it was a lovely morning they decided to take their bikes. The air was warm and sweet-smelling, and the verges of the lanes were foaming with cow parsley. As they pedalled along, Ben wondered what this Aurora girl would be like.

Chris's house was surrounded by trees and couldn't be seen from the lane. However, at the little turning leading to it there was a carved wooden sign saying TIMBERTOPS and next to it something that looked like a miniature mail van fixed to a post. It was made of wood and freshly painted a glossy red.

'Must be a postbox,' said Ben.

'Spot on.' The reply came from Chris himself who was striding towards them, a wide smile on his tanned face. 'Just came down to collect the mail, actually. Take a look inside.' Ben opened the hinged roof and lifted out the letters.

'Supercool, Chris. Never seen one like this.'

'Can't take any credit myself. Rory's just finished it.'

Who's Rory? thought Ben, puzzled.

'Well, welcome, both of you. You've come just at the right moment, actually. We're about to have a fry-up. Can you manage a late breakfast?'

'Thanks, Chris. Actually we've had breakfast already . . .' Gramps caught sight of Ben's face. 'But if you're talking fry-up I'm sure we could find room.'

'I'm just sorting things in the kitchen. Go around to the back, Ben. You'll find Rory . . . there.' He finished to the air. Ben had vanished.

When Ben looked around the garden there was no one to be seen. The only sign of life was the blackened remains of a fire with three short sawn-off logs standing on end next to it. He went closer to inspect and found an old black frying pan and a toasting fork. No need for detective skills to work out that people had been sitting on the logs and cooking on the camp fire. With any luck this was where breakfast would be cooked too. OK, but where was Rory?

Suddenly he heard a voice above his head. 'Hi. You can come up if you like.'

The voice seemed to be coming from high in branches of the old oak tree, but Ben couldn't see anyone hidden in the foliage. And even the lowest branches of the tree were so high off the ground that he couldn't see how anyone could have got up there.

'We're here,' called the voice. Yes, it was definitely coming from up in the tree. Ben was looking hard for a sign of movement when he thought he saw two pairs of green eyes just visible through the screen of leaves. Yes, one pair belonged to a large marmalade cat but the other pair belonged to a person. A girl's face now poked out of the foliage. It was pale, freckled and surrounded by a mass of red hair.

'You must be Ben,' she said.

Ben just nodded, too mystified to speak. Who was this wild-haired girl? If she was Aurora, she was nothing like the Aurora he'd imagined.

'So, do you want to come up, then?'

Of course he wanted to come up. The question was how? There weren't any branches within reach. How on earth had she done it? No help for it. He'd have to ask her. But her face had disappeared and he'd no idea how he was going to reach her.

Suddenly he heard, 'Stand back,' as something fell from the tree, unrolling as it did so to reveal itself to be a very nifty, handmade-looking rope ladder.

I suppose Wonder Girl has made this as well, Ben thought. But was it strong enough to take his weight? He'd only seen her face. She might be much smaller and lighter than him. He was much too curious to hesitate long, though.

The ladder swayed around a bit as he climbed so that the bottom of it kept crashing against the tree. Ben was too determined to find this girl to let that worry him, though. Looking up he saw that some old planks of wood had been fixed to two sturdy side branches. When he arrived at the top of the rope ladder, he was expecting to see the redheaded girl on this platform. Instead he found a little structure – half tepee, half tree house – perched on it.

Some old green tarpaulin had been suspended from the branch above the platform and attached to lower branches to form this sort of tree tent. 'Hi. You must be Ben, right?' she said, opening the flap wider to make room for him to come inside.

'Wow. I mean yeah.' Ben's face had lit up with wonder as he looked around in the green-tinted half-light. He'd always wanted a tree house, but there wasn't even a tree in his tiny garden at home.

'And you? Are you Aurora?'

'I'm Rory.'

Ben blinked. 'You made the postbox then. But, Rory – isn't that a boy's name?'

'Usually. But if you've been given a pants name like Aurora . . .'

'I get it.' Ben laughed.

'I'm not sure you do. Fact is my mum's a dancer. Her name was Philippa Potts. When she joined the National Ballet Company, they suggested she changed it. So she called herself Carina. And she'd met my father who was a violinist in the orchestra. His name is Luigi Crimona. So there you are – drumroll – Carina Crimona.'

'Wow,' said Ben, trying not to laugh.

Rory rolled her eyes at him. 'She jokes she only married my dad for his name and it's true they didn't stay together very long. They split up when I was very small and he travels all over the world so I don't see him that often.'

'And so you're really . . .'

'Yep – Aurora Crimona. Mum was expecting me to become a ballerina like her. Had to dash her hopes, though. Even if I had the talent, which I most definitely don't, you have to be crazily dedicated. Such hard work and you get sprains and blisters and all sorts. Definitely not for me. Then there's all the touring,' she added. Her face had become sad. Ben caught on immediately.

'So you're with Chris for the summer, are you?'

'Yes. Mum and I used to come together for a week or two, but this time I'm by myself with Chris. Mum's coming for a weekend towards the end of the holiday, though. And I'm not complaining. Chris and I are having a good time together.'

'He helped you with this, I bet.' Sitting in the leafy light of the tree house, Ben was thinking how much he'd love to have one himself.

'Of course he helped. You don't think he'd let me use his saw, do you? But it was my idea and I did most of the nailing. And I put up the hooks and things.'

The hooks had been fixed on to the tree trunk, and suspended on them were a water bottle, a string bag containing some apples, a packet of crisps and a bow and arrow. Ben stared at the bow, unable to keep a broad grin off his face.

'What do you shoot?' he asked. There was a brief pause.

'Well, I haven't actually managed to shoot anything yet. And, anyway, they don't have metal tips on so I couldn't kill anything. But when there's nobody around I aim at the pigeons.'

They looked down to see two fat ones strutting around on the grass.

'At least I manage to give them a good fright. They're always after Chris's fruit. You can have a go after breakfast if you like. So, what do you do when you stay with your grandpa?'

'Hmm... well, we go fishing and I help him with his bees and...' Ben paused, trying to think of something as awesome as her tree house to tell her about.

'And I'm investigating why so many bees are disappearing. You know, like a detective. I don't normally tell people that, of course.' He was enjoying the way Rory was now looking at him intently.

'And I turned into a bee myself for a while – for my investigation.'

At this Rory snorted. 'You're having a laugh, aren't you? Humans don't turn into bees, in case you didn't know.'

'No, really, I did.' *Why did I open my big mouth?* he was thinking. 'Well look, to be honest, it wasn't actually intentional. I ate some of Gramps's royal jelly and then – whoosh! – I shrivelled and shrank into a bee.'

'Yeah, right,' laughed Rory. 'Not been reading *Alice in Wonderland* by any chance?'

'Okay, forget it.' Ben thought for a moment, then continued. 'To be honest, if you told me you'd been a bee, I probably wouldn't believe you either. Anyway, the other thing my grandpa and I are going to be doing is organising a Big BuzZ – sort of like a garden fête but with lots of activities to help people understand why bees are disappearing. We want to make it fun too. Lots of games and races and things.' He paused. 'You any good at organising games?'

'I'm pretty good at face painting actually. Like a face-painting stand? I could do bee faces.'

'Brilliant! You know what – my grandpa's been on at me to go on a demonstration against pesticides with him. Well, it's a march, really. I thought it would be a bit of a drag, but what

if you painted our faces and we dressed up as bees?'

'So you're mad keen on bees, then.' Rory was grinning at him. 'And of course you've seen Chris's top bar hives – the ones he made himself?'

'No,' said Ben, wondering what Rory knew of Chris and Gramps's somewhat competitive attitude when it came to beekeeping. 'Gramps did mention them, but I've never seen them.'

'Gosh. You have to come and look. They're really neat. You know, in ordinary hives the bees build their combs in those square frames that come with the hive. But with top bar hives there aren't any frames. There's just, like, these bars resting across the top of the hive. It means the bees can build their comb in any shape they like – like wild bees do. Just wait till you see what they do! But the *really* great thing for us is that he's put a glass panel in the side so that you can actually see what the bees are up to inside.'

'Wow, that's so great for people who've never been inside a hive and . . .' Ben stopped, noticing Rory's quizzical expression.

'And I'd love to see them,' he finished enthusiastically. 'Can we? Right now?'

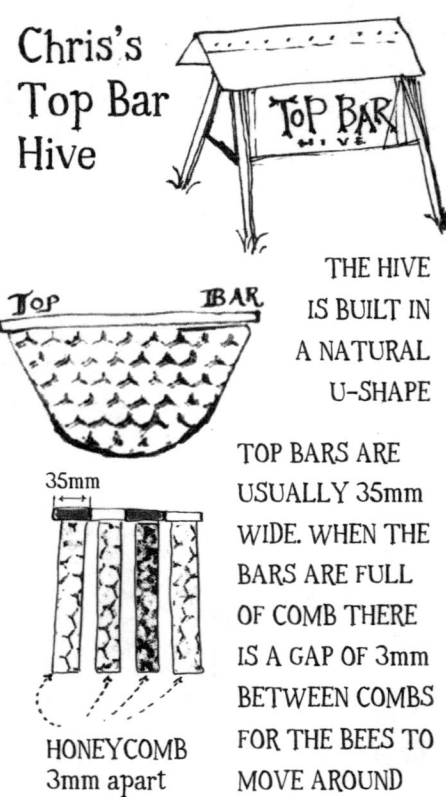

Chris's Top Bar Hive

THE HIVE IS BUILT IN A NATURAL U-SHAPE

TOP BARS ARE USUALLY 35mm WIDE. WHEN THE BARS ARE FULL OF COMB THERE IS A GAP OF 3mm BETWEEN COMBS FOR THE BEES TO MOVE AROUND

HONEYCOMB 3mm apart

'No, you'll need to come back later. Night-time's best for looking inside. Then you can shine a torch and watch them. In the day you can't really see anything because it's dark inside the hive.'

You're telling me, thought Ben, remembering his surprise when he'd first crawled through the little hole into the hive and into the darkness. This time, though, he kept his thoughts to himself.

'Well,' said Rory, 'we should probably see what those two are doing about breakfast. I'm starving.' They poked their heads out of the tarpaulin and saw that Gramps and Chris had got the fire going again.

'We're coming down to fry the sausages' she called to them. She nudged Ben, 'Come on, follow me.'

'That's it. I can't explain it,' Gramps was saying. 'I mean, if it didn't really happen, if it was a dream, where did he get all that information? It's all the latest research, as you know, not something they'd tell you at school.'

'What?' Chris's jaw had dropped in astonishment. 'Toby, you can't be telling me you believe . . .' Chris stopped when he caught of Ben and Rory approaching – but too late for Ben not to have heard what he was saying and to have guessed what he was talking about.

Ben decided, however, to pretend he hadn't heard anything. He'd had just about enough of trying to convince people of his transformation. Let them believe whatever they liked.

So, instead of joining them, he went off to pick up another log from Chris's log pile to add to the three around the fire.

Rory already had the sausages sizzling and spluttering in the pan when he returned.

'Chris, Ben's really dying to see your special hive,' she was saying.

Ben looked to see what Gramps made of that, but luckily he didn't seem put out and just carried on slicing mushrooms.

'Well, how about you come up tonight after supper, then, Ben? Best to take advantage of the good weather. They've forecasted a storm for tomorrow and we can't do it in thunder and rain.'

Gramps slipped the mushrooms into the pan. 'Thanks, Chris. I've never seen the bees at night either. You're on.'

As soon as Rory had served the sausages, eggs and mushrooms, she turned to Chris. 'You know that old wooden bow at the back of the shed? If we put a new string on it, Ben and I could have some target practice after breakfast.'

'That's a real bow, Rory, and a good bit larger than the one you've been using.'

'Oh, I'll be fine with it,' said Ben, trying to give the impression he was an experienced archer without actually saying so. Chris didn't look at all convinced.

When everybody had finished eating and the last scrap of egg yolk had been mopped up with the fried bread, Ben, eager to find the bow, started gathering up the plates without being asked and took them into the kitchen.

Unfortunately washing up wasn't as quick as it would have been at Gramps's. Chris was the type who likes the plates rinsed so clean before they get into the dishwasher that Ben wondered why he bothered to use one at all.

He noticed Rory looking at him. Her mouth was firmly straight, but her sparkling eyes were a giveaway. She was definitely suppressing a grin.

Ben raised his eyebrows in Rory's direction and turned back to Chris, adopting his polite this-is-so-fascinating expression as if a lecture on the advanced theory of dishwasher loading was just what he and Gramps had come over for.

Luckily, with four of them on the job, the kitchen was soon gleaming.

'I'll take a look at this while you fix up that bow,' said Gramps, picking up a newspaper and settling into a chair, soon oblivious of everybody and everything.

Chapter Thirteen

'I should have told your grandpa that paper is a week old,' said Chris as the three of them walked down to the end of the garden.

'Shouldn't worry,' said Ben. 'He'll be fine. As long as it's any kind of print he's happy. He'd probably sit and read the back of a cereal packet if there were no books or papers around. Comes of being born before screens were invented.' He stopped suddenly. Had he offended Chris?

But Chris just laughed and disappeared into the shed and this time Rory made no attempt to hide her own amusement. Both of them giggling, they followed Chris.

Ben had been wondering why finding the bow would require so much hunting. If Chris's workshop was anything like his kitchen, the bow would be fixed neatly to the wall under a label:

> Bow, Spare, Old and
> In Need of Attention.

The interior of the shed was a bit dim after the bright sunshine. As Ben's eyes became used to the light he saw that it was he'd expected, a very orderly workshop. Chris's tools were all ranged on separate pegs on the wall and little plastic drawers contained a variety of nails and screws.

Chris headed towards the back of the shed, which looked like a treasure trove of all sorts of unwanted or outgrown equipment from an ancient baby pram and rusty metal lawn mower, to tricycles, antique clothes wringers and old highchairs.

'Shocking mess, isn't it, Ben?' apologised Chris 'It isn't even my stuff. But when you've got a shed your relatives seem to think you'll be happy to keep things that "might come in useful one day".'

Ben could see that this glorious collection of discarded stuff would be a very exciting place to poke around in . . . sometime. But how long was it going take to uncover a bow in all this muddle?

Suddenly something in the far corner caught his eye. Some sort of sixth sense was alerted by the letters: **pons** printed clearly on some cardboard. Pons? In a matter of seconds he was in that corner excitedly holding up a dusty box clearly labelled **Assorted weapons**.

The box was quite heavy and he put it down quickly to have a proper look. It was full of shields, swords, Roman helmets, belts with daggers and . . .

Ben stopped investigating and put on a Viking helmet, turning to face Rory, a curved and menacing Saracen sword in his hand.

Rory ignored him. She darted forward and triumphantly seized the wooden bow that was poking up from one corner of the box.

'Come on, Ben. This is it. Look, it's even got some arrows taped on to it. Chris, could you show us how to put on another string? No, actually, Ben, you do the string with Chris and I'll go and set up the target.' She disappeared.

'Well, that's us organised,' said Chris, inspecting the bow as he spoke.

Ben might have been irritated at Rory making all the decisions if he hadn't realised that fixing the bow and watching Chris handling it might give him some idea of how to hold the thing and then, possibly, shoot with it – hopefully without letting on that he'd never held any kind of bow before. And this one was a good bit bigger than Rory's. Clearly Chris was having similar thoughts.

'You know, Ben, I'm a bit concerned about you using this. You're what – eleven? I'd already had some experience with bows and must have been about thirteen when I used it.' He was eying Ben up and down thoughtfully as he spoke. 'Tell you what. I'll fix the string anyway and I'll let you try and, worst-way, I'll keep it here for you for a year or two. How about that?'

Ben clamped his mouth shut to stop himself telling Chris what he thought about that. Eventually he forced out a reply in his best being-polite-to-people-you've-just-met manner.

'Er, okay, then, Chris, but I think you'll see I can manage.' His voice was confident but, watching Chris deftly re-stringing the very large and professional-looking bow, that was the last thing he felt.

Satisfied with his work, Chris looked around for an arrow. 'Nicely made, eh, Ben? The bow was from an archery shop, but we made extra arrows ourselves. Okay, let's try it outside.'

Ben was secretly relieved to find that Chris's 'let's try it' seemed to mean that Chris was having a go first.

'Plenty of space, eh, Ben?' said Chris, surveying the scene. 'No risk of hitting anyone. Right, that oak tree will make a good target.'

It took three attempts before Chris managed to hit the tree. None too pleased, he went off to collect the arrows.

'My turn now,' Ben said to himself as he picked up the bow and lifted it to shoulder height as he'd seen Chris do.

Chris returned with the arrows and Ben waited for him to hand him one. But Chris was holding them firmly.

'Ben, I'm sorry about this, but as soon as I saw that bow I should have warned you straight away that it's much bigger than I remembered—'

'It's Okay – I'm tall for my age.'

Chris ignored the interruption and continued: 'And much more powerful. And what about the arrows? Really sharp. I doubt children are allowed to use them nowadays. Very dangerous if they went off target and hit an animal or a human. Besides they are not meant for the sort of target Rory has. You'd need something like a sack of hay with a target stuck on to it.'

'But we could make one of those and I'd be really careful.'

'Sorry, Ben, but I don't think it's a good idea. Look, let me just speak to your grandpa and see what he says. Why don't you go and see what Rory is up to?' Without giving Ben a chance to reply, Chris set off briskly towards the house.

Oh yes, thought Ben, *great escape tactic! Go and ask Gramps and that'll be two against one.* It was pretty obvious whose side Gramps would be on.

Perhaps he'd go and see where Rory had disappeared to. There was no sign of her in the garden. She was supposed to have been setting up the target, so possibly she'd found a good place in the field. He found her there, half hidden in the long grass, in front of a little plastic target.

'Hi, Rory,' he said. She looked up.

'I didn't hear you coming. I was just checking . . .' She stuck her mobile in her pocket.

'How did it go? You've been ages.' Then she noticed his expression and that there was no bow in his hand.

'Oh. Chris couldn't manage to re-string it, then?'

'He managed fine.'

'And how did you find it?' Looking at Ben's face again, she immediately regretted the question. 'It is much bigger and heavier and probably a lot harder to handle than mine,' she said sympathetically.

'Well, I wouldn't know, would I?' said Ben bitterly.

Luckily Rory was quick on the uptake. 'Oh no, don't tell me he went all health and safety on you. Let me guess. "I'm really sorry, Ben, but I can't possibly let you use it. It's much too dangerous. You could really hurt someone with that." Right?'

'Dead right,' said Ben. 'And now he's gone off to get Gramps to side with him.'

'He was just the same about me using the saw when I made the post box. He did all the easy things with the electric saw and left all the really hard things with hand tools to me. And I could see how easy it was with the saw. Just like slicing butter. And, anyway, how are you supposed to learn if you never get to try?'

'Exactly.'

'How about we have a go with mine just to start with? We can take turns. I've got enough arrows. And when you've had a bit of practice we can both go and try to persuade them.'

Ben looked at the bow she was offering. Rory was being so decent offering to share it that he didn't want to let on that for him it was now just a flimsy bit of plastic.

He took it from her and took aim. Satisfyingly, whilst the arrow was nowhere near the bullseye, it had hit the board. He picked up a second arrow and again it hit the board – this time on an outer ring.

'Wow, well done, Ben. Carry on a minute and I'll go and get us a drink and see what the old crumblies are up to.'

Ben picked up the third arrow and again it hit the board and even nearer the centre. He certainly had a talent for archery.

Cheered up now, Ben sat down in the grass for a moment, just happy to be in the warm, humming air. Hey, how could have he been so obsessed with bows and arrows that he hadn't even noticed Chris's bees? Now, with their familiar buzzing in his ears, he felt very contented. He looked around the meadow

and saw that, hidden in the undergrowth, were a number of unusual bee hives – lower and wider than Gramps's hives.

Suddenly, beyond the hives, someone strange in the neighbour's field caught his eye. A strange, bulky figure wearing a bright red check shirt and a funny sort of hat. Not a human surely. Ben laughed. Of course. An outsize scarecrow. Filled with straw. Perfect. Grinning with delight, Ben was already racing back to retrieve Chris's bow.

Okay, the bow was rather large for him, but he'd had plenty of practice with Rory's now and so he confidently placed the arrow on its rest and raised the bow to shoulder height.

'Hey, Ben, what are you up to?' Rory was back, carrying a tray.

'I've just found the perfect target – the scarecrow,' he called.

Rory's voice was horrified as she shouted back, 'That isn't a scarecrow—'

But the arrow was already winging its way across the field. It was flying lower than Ben had intended, but still there was a satisfying thud as it hit his target.

A howl of pain and indignation came from the figure.

'That's Stringfellow!'

They stood in shock as the arrow fell to the ground and the figure turned round, his ruddy face almost the colour of his shirt.

'What b-b-bloody s-stupid hoodlum—?'

Chapter Fourteen

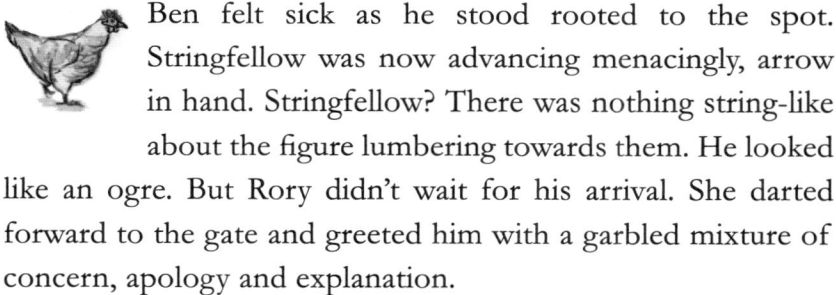 Ben felt sick as he stood rooted to the spot. Stringfellow was now advancing menacingly, arrow in hand. Stringfellow? There was nothing string-like about the figure lumbering towards them. He looked like an ogre. But Rory didn't wait for his arrival. She darted forward to the gate and greeted him with a garbled mixture of concern, apology and explanation.

'. . . his first go with that bow, you know . . . never meant to . . . Is it terribly painful?'

Rory and the giant man were standing at the gate as Rory finished her explanation. Ben nervously approached them.

'Ah ha, so you m-m-mistook me for a scarecrow, d-did you?' Stringfellow's voice was every bit as deep and menacing as the ogre's in Jack in the Beanstalk. 'Well, that does m-make me feel a great deal better about having an arrow shot into my b-b-backside. You know what should happen to you? You should be put into the s-s-stocks and pelted with rotten eggs as an example to other unruly young wretches who don't know how to b-behave themselves. Just wait till I speak to—"

But the last thing Rory wanted to do was wait until Stringfellow had dobbed them in to whichever adult he was intending to speak.

'Just sit down a minute first, Stringfellow, and I'll get you a drink. You must be feeling very shocked,' she said, looking at him with deep concern.

'Young l-lady, I really don't know what you are d-doing associating with such a dangerous hooligan.'

Ben and Rory were both relieved to see, however, that, whilst speaking, Stringfellow was gradually manoeuvring his great bulk earthwards. He grimaced again as his bottom reached the ground – but he accepted the drink Rory was now offering.

'He certainly isn't a hooligan, Stringfellow. It was a complete accident, like I said.' She passed him a biscuit. 'He's actually here doing very important work saving bees. Why don't you tell him what you've been doing, Ben?'

Ben realised this was a ploy to distract Stringfellow. Nevertheless, the last thing he wanted to do was to explain his transformation to a strange adult who clearly took a very dim view of him. Stringfellow was not in any case ready to be distracted so easily and waved his finger at Ben.

'Thank heavens these d-dungarees are such thick denim or I could have ended up in hospital.'

'I'm sorry,'

'It's a great mercy you're such an ap-p-palling shot or I might have had that arrow in my b-back and that would have been exceedingly dangerous.'

'Really, really sorry.'

Stringfellow was silent for a moment, munching on his second biscuit. Rory decided that, as he didn't seem to be in pain now, it was about time to divert his attention. She'd been bursting with curiosity about what had really happened to Ben ever since he'd first told her the story about his transformation. He'd clammed up straight away, though, and she couldn't resist this opportunity to get him to talk.

'Come on, Ben, tell us how you managed to turn into a bee to investigate.'

Stringfellow's mouth fell open again – but this time not because he was about to consume a biscuit.

'Good heavens, young m-man. Are you asking us to believe that you have extraordinary p-powers?'

'Er, not exactly. It was the royal jelly, really. It all happened when I ate some. I transformed, you see, into a bee. I mean not suddenly, just like that. First, I could feel myself shrinking and I had prickly feelings where hair was growing on me and then I looked at my arm, but it wasn't an arm anymore, and then suddenly I was tiny and on the floor . . .'

He went on to tell them that, though he'd been frightened, it had occurred to him that maybe, as a bee, he would be able to solve the mystery of Gramps's missing bees and how he'd decided to try to enter a hive. How once there he'd discovered that the bees were in great danger from a new illness.

It was a dying bee who'd gasped out the information that he was seeking – what was causing the bees to get ill? On the brink of death, she'd warned him of the danger of oilseed rape and then had gasped 'beware the Oppies', before falling on her back, stone dead.

Rory and Stringfellow stared at Ben in wordless wonder. It was very satisfying. But when, finally, he reached the part where the hornet was hovering over his bed Rory could keep silent no longer. 'Holy cow, that must have been terrifying! How did you manage to get away?'

Ben didn't answer immediately. Get away? He hadn't actually got away, had he? He remembered Gramps coming into the room but what had happened to the hornet?

He realised that their next question would probably be how he'd changed back. A question to which he had no answer.

To his great relief he heard Gramps's voice calling.

'Seb, wouldn't you like to sit somewhere more comfortable and have a cup of coffee with us?'

'I'm b-being very well entertained here, thank you. Impressive young m-man, your grandson.' Rory and Ben exchanged a relieved grin as Chris and Gramps came and joined them on the grass.

'Yes, I gather he's got some new information on why bees are vanishing.'

He was interrupted by Rory. 'Hey, Chris. Bet you didn't know exactly why bees are getting ill and dying but Ben does.' And she was off on an account of what the dying bee had told Ben.

'Hmm,' said Chris when she'd finished. 'Never heard of a human turning into a bee myself. Didn't know bees could talk, come to that. But what you say this back-to-front bee said about them losing their navigational skills – well, that is what certain scientists have been reporting for some while.'

Rory broke in excitedly. 'But if people actually know there are pesticides that kill bees, how come the farmers carry on using them? Why hasn't the government banned them?'

'Right,' agreed Ben. He turned to Gramps. 'It's just what I asked you yesterday, remember? You said it was complicated.'

'There is a one-word answer,' said Chris wryly. 'Can anyone guess?'

'Money,' replied Ben, remembering Gramps's explanation. 'That's it, isn't it, Chris?'

'Money indeed, Rory. Neonicotinoids are enormously profitable. And that makes the companies who manufacture them extremely powerful.'

Ben looked puzzled. 'Not more powerful than the government, surely?'

'Wish that were true,' said Chris darkly.

'You see,' said Gramps, 'with all the money they have, it's easy for the agrochemical companies to pay their own scientists to cast doubt on the research of those who are blaming the neonicotinoids for the bee losses. They'd say, for instance, that there isn't sufficient proof. It's got a name that kind of thing, you know – industry-friendly science. D'you get it?'

Rory and Ben nodded.

'And it's not just the manufacturers of neonicotinoids either,' continued Gramps. 'There are companies selling all kinds of products used in agriculture and in gardens and parks, too, which have serious side-effects – things like glyphosates. ❋ And not only on insects. On humans as well.'

Ben interrupted Gramps excitedly. 'Whoa! It's just like tobacco, isn't it? It's, like, everyone knows that cigarettes cause cancer and other illnesses where people die horribly, but the government doesn't actually ban them.'

'Not only that, the power of the tobacco lobby was – or is – so enormous that it took a very long time before governments would even admit there was a link between smoking and dying of cancer.'

'What's a lobby, ❋ Toby?' asked Rory but before he had a chance to answer Chris broke in.

'Yes, and Big Tobacco is so powerful that, even when the link between smoking and death from lung cancer was exposed and, as a result, cigarette sales started to fall – well, the tobacco industry just spent astronomic sums of money to reassure the public. They were so successful that the sales of tobacco actually rose again.'

'Right, now I've got it, Gramps. Big Chemicals, Big Tobacco – it's they that are, like, the Evil Powers you talked about last night.'

'Did I?' said Gramps, puzzled.

'Yes, Gramps, you did. Remember, you said that ordinary people can prevent the Triumph of Evil, but only if they take action.'

Chris and Seb were exchanging grins.

'So you're turning your grandson into an activist,' said Seb. 'You'll be getting him on that march soon.'

'Rory might come too.' Ben turned to her. 'How about if you come we wear T-shirts saying **Ban Neonics – Now and Forever!**? We could get some printed and sell them at the Big BuzZ.'

'Tell you what,' said Stringfellow, 'you could get me one of those T-shirts.' Ben and Rory looked at him to see if he was joking.

'Yes. I m-mean it. Get me one too. Hoarding size I'd need. Very ef-fective on a march.'

Ben looked at his broad chest and grinned. 'Stringfellow – who gave you that nickname?' he asked.

'It's my surname actually. My real name is Sebastian. But certain people,' he said, looking at Rory, 'use it as my f-first name too.'

'Well, it is funny isn't it? I mean it isn't exactly the most appropriate name. You should swap with your friend who does look like a bean pole. It's Barty, isn't it?'

'Barty Broadbeam do you mean?' asked Chris. But as he was speaking his eyes had wandered to his bow and arrow, which still lay where Ben had dropped them to the ground. Chris raised his eyebrows at him.

'Thought we left those near my workshop. How've they found themselves over here?'

Sitting between Chris and Stringfellow, Ben had no idea

what to say and felt his face going red. But, before he had a chance to answer, Stringfellow was already speaking.

'Ah yes, Chris. These arrows. I'm s-surprised you use them with children around. D-don't know what these arrowheads are made of but they look sharp enough. It's a good thing they're not actually m-metal. Even so – they c-could really hurt someone. If you're teaching Ben to shoot, why don't you get some with rubber tips off the internet? Then he can aim at t-targets instead of –' he paused for what seemed an endless moment – 't-trees or whatever.'

Chris was frowning as he turned to Ben.

This is it, thought Ben. *Now he's going to say that he'd told me not to touch the bow and arrows so how had they moved.*

But, miraculously, before Chris had a chance to say anything Gramps piped up cheerily, 'Tell you what, folks, we should really be getting back now and, as Chris was kind enough to look out his old bow for Ben, perhaps we should look into getting the tips. We can report back later.'

'Yes, we're going to be looking into Chris's hives as soon as it gets dark. Want to come over, Stringfellow?' asked Rory.

'I should be delighted, young lady.'

'Had a good time?' Gramps asked as they cycled home.

'Now it's you who's sounding smug, Gramps. Must be something they put in the water round here. But, yes, I did. Rory and Stringfellow are really cool. It's great they're coming on the march, isn't it?'

'Yes, with those two as allies, your bee-saving campaign is getting off to a good start.'

'You know the conversation we were having about multi-national companies, Gramps? Just when I asked you about the evil powers, Seb got us on to the subject of the march and you never answered. It is those big businesses you meant, though, isn't it?'

'What I thought I'd said last night is that in James Bond films you usually have a powerful and ruthless villain intent on world domination, but he's defeated almost singlehandedly by a fearless hero with very lethal gadgets!'

'Yes, and then you said that in real life it's usually the evil powers who triumph. Is that because there are so many of them seeking world domination?'

'Well, you could say they have that already. No, what the multi-national companies are actually seeking is ever greater profits and there are some of them that are quite as ruthless as any James Bond villain in their pursuit of those profits.'

'That can't be true, Gramps. They'd have the government and the police after them, wouldn't they?'

'Let's just say we don't, as yet, have adequate laws to prevent large companies endangering human lives and destroying the environment.'

'So how can protest marches help defeat them?'

'All depends on numbers, doesn't it, Ben? If enough people turn up and there's enough publicity in the papers and on television, it might encourage governments to stand up to big business. Politicians want to be re-elected, so they want to be seen to be doing what they think most electors want. And there are other things as well. We've all got the power of purchase for instance.'

'The power of purchase? I don't get that, Gramps.'

'That means buying from companies who do care for the environment and don't disregard the health risks to humans and wildlife of the products they manufacture. If you're not part of the solution, you're part of the problem as far as I'm concerned. No use blaming everything on governments and multinationals. So being careful of what we buy is one thing we can do. But there are all sorts of ways. Bet you and Rory can think of your own.'

'She is pretty impressive, isn't she?'

'So not such a sparkly type, after all, then?'

'Wrong, Gramps. Didn't you notice she's got green sparkly toenails? And she's going to paint mine too.'

Chapter Fifteen

It was Rory who opened the door. 'Come through and see,' she greeted them. 'Chris has found the gun.'

Ben was a bit mystified by her words, but followed her through to the kitchen where they found Stringfellow already installed drinking tea. Gramps put the flapjacks they'd brought on the table.

'Toby, you know that gun I mentioned to you?' said Chris. 'Here it is. You're welcome to borrow it and see if it helps.'

He handed Gramps a white plastic pistol with a curly tube for a nozzle. Not exactly the air rifle Ben had been imagining, but rather intriguing all the same.

'You fill it with icing sugar like I said and you spray the whole frame with the nozzle – one side at a time. The bees end up looking like little snow bees. Cute sight.'

Gramps caught Ben's bemused expression. 'I forgot to tell you, Ben. Chris said he'd lend me this. Just might help my remaining bees, he reckons.'

'All I can say is that when I use it I find the floor underneath the combs covered with dead varroa. Very satisfying.'

'How does the sugar kill them, Chris? Deadly to varroa is it?'

'The icing sugar is very fine and the bees, to get it off them, have to start grooming themselves and each other very vigorously. The result is that the varroa are brushed off the bees' backs and end up on the floor of the hive. They can't fly – so that's curtains for them.'

Rory made fists in the air and shook them. 'Wahey, death to varroa!'

Ben imitated her. 'Wahey, down with all those who harm bees!' They got to their feet and started a war-dance, chanting, shaking their fists in the air and stamping their feet.

Chris needed to raise his voice to speak.

'Toby, I've one concern. This gun works in my top-bar hives because I can easily pull out the combs and spray them, but I'm not sure how it will work in yours.'

Gramps's face stiffened. 'Back to that are you, Chris? "Top-bar hives are better for bee health . . . I've hardly lost any of my bees . . ." Hasn't it ever occurred to you that the real reason your bees are all okay could be that the farmers round here aren't using neonicotinoids?'

His raised voice penetrated Rory and Ben's war dance. They stopped to look curiously at the two men and saw that Gramps's face was red.

Uh-oh, thought Ben. *Here we go again.*

Knowing how easily his grandfather took offence, he feared that the next thing would be that he'd snatch up his car keys and, bingo, that would be the end of the night visit to the hives.

 see page 217

Distract him quickly, he thought, but, before he had a chance to say anything, Chris spoke.

'Look, Toby, I'm with you. There's no kind of hive that's able to protect bees from neonicotinoids. What's more, we live far enough apart that if they have been used by a farmer near you it wouldn't have affected my bees anyway. But with all the things that are menacing bee life, well, I suppose I just like to think I'm giving mine the best chance of survival by letting them live in the most natural way.'

Gramps's face relaxed. Ben seized the moment to ask the question he'd had on his mind since they'd all started talking about the neonicotinoids.

'Gramps,' he asked, 'if Fred Bart is bee friendly now, who do you think might be killing your bees? You must have some idea.'

'I have my suspicions, but how can I prove anything? You know that bees travel big distances collecting nectar. Beyond Fred's farm is the Broadacres estate. Massive farm. I know for a fact a lot of spraying goes on there.'

With a horrified voice, Rory jumped into the conversation. 'That can't be right. I know the family who live at Broadacres. I ride with Vanessa. She lends me one of their horses. And her father's really nice. It can't be them,' she finished firmly.

The men looked at each other awkwardly, not quite sure how to continue the conversation.

'Her father may be nice to *you* . . .' said Ben, thinking of Gramps's lost bees and the danger his friends were in, but seeing Rory's upset face he decided not to carry on – not now, anyway.

'It's nearly dark. Shall we go and see the bees now, Chris?'

'You're on, Ben. I'll grab some torches.'

In a few minutes they were back in Chris's field. Just as in Gramps's field, there were hives dotted about here and there. But Chris clearly had a particular one in mind.

'They were up to something rather wonderful when I took a peep yesterday. Hope they're still at it today.'

As Chris released the catch of the door of the observation window Gramps and Sam held back to allow Rory and Ben the first look. Chris handed a torch to them and they peered in.

The bees might have just come inside the hive after a long day of foraging, but there was no sense of them settling down for the night. The combs were just one heaving mass of bees, layers thick, clambering over each other in perpetual movement.

Ben couldn't help grinning.

'What's so funny?' asked Rory, who had been expecting awe and wonder rather than Ben's evident amusement.

'Not funny exactly,' he whispered, not wanting Chris to hear. 'It's just watching them climbing over each other like that reminds me of what it felt like to be in a great mass of bees like that. Jolly weird the first time, I can tell you. You're going one way. They're going another.'

'Like rush hour, then,' said Rory.

'Exactly – only nobody minds being jostled. It's like being part of one big body.'

'What's that about rush hour?' asked Chris.

'Just saying that's what it looks like in there.'

'Well come down to this end and I'll show you the truly wondrous thing. Can you see? Because the combs hang vertically you mostly only see the sides of them, but, with this last one, if you look carefully, you can see the whole comb.'

Ben and Rory peered again. Yes, this time they could see the whole of the comb, covered like the others with a dense, moving carpet of bees. But as for the comb itself . . .

'Wow,' Ben exclaimed, 'it's kind of heart-shaped. Is that the wondrous thing?'

'Anything else? Towards the bottom?'

'Holy cow, Chris. How on earth are they doing that?'

Ben followed Rory's gaze to the very bottom of the comb where strings of bees were clinging to each other and, with no support but each other, hanging in the air in looping strands.

'How indeed! It is quite amazing, isn't it?'

'But why are they doing that?' asked Ben, who had enough experience of bee life to know there was very little time for play. If bees were hanging in the air making themselves into living ropes –well, they weren't practising their circus skills!

'People have been studying bees for hundreds of years, but,

you know what, Ben, these insects still keep some of their secrets. People have their theories why, but even scientists aren't sure.'

'Want to give Seb and me a look, you two?' said Gramps.

Ben and Rory reluctantly withdrew their noses from the glass.

Gramps bent down to look and when he exclaimed, 'Oh my goodness, Chris!' his voice was just as excited as Ben's and Rory's had been. 'You know, I've seen bees festooning before, but never anything on this scale.'

'It's sort of like bee lace, isn't it, Seb?' said Rory as Seb, too, bent down to look. Chris turned to Gramps.

'Know what, Toby, let's leave them to it for a minute while I show you something in that hive behind the tree over there that might be of interest to you.'

Ben's ears pricked up. This sounded as if it might be interesting to him too and he followed the two men.

Before they even reached the tree, Ben noticed something. The air was filled with the hum of bees buzzing, but it was not the happy-sounding buzz Ben was used to. No, this sound had something urgent and anxious about it.

'They sound agitated, Chris.'

'Exactly. And that's why I wanted you to have a peep inside.' He opened the flap as he spoke and moved out of the way for Ben and Gramps to look.

'But you can't see anything. It's just black . . . well, black and moving. A solid wall of bees, isn't it? All over the glass.' Ben paused. 'I know. They're about to swarm, aren't they? Gramps told me once they get very agitated before they swarm.'

'Spot on, Ben. The hive is getting overfull, you see, and they're ready to split off into a new colony. All they're waiting for is a new queen to be ready. Then they'll fly off with the old queen. But, as you see, they're not very good at waiting. Anyway, Toby, that's where you come in. I was wondering if you'd like the new swarm?'

There was silence for a moment.

'Don't think I don't appreciate the offer, Chris. But it's not going to work, is it? I mean, I presume what you usually do is take out the comb with the old queen on it and put it in a new empty hive. But there's no way your top-bar comb is going to fit into one of my hives.'

'Ha, but my offer is better than that. We'll put the queen comb in a new top-bar hive. I've just made one and you're welcome to take it and try. Call it a loan. See how you like it. If you do and you want to keep it – well, you can just help me make another one for here.'

He grinned at Gramps and Ben couldn't suppress a grin either as Gramps gave Chris a friendly pat on the back.

'Very generous offer. Thanks, Chris. Really happy to give it a try.'

'Well, if that's all agreed, I suggest we collect the other two and go and attack those flapjacks now.'

Chapter Sixteen

The first thing Ben's eyes went to as he came back into the kitchen was the sugar gun on the kitchen table. Why had no one thought of making a really large version? Imagine spraying people and turning them into sugary snowmen!

'Gramps, how about a larger version of the sugar gun to spray humans? How wicked would that be!'

'Yeah!' Rory agreed. 'And we could have it at the Big BuzZ. Just like paintballing! People would pay to shoot at each other. Wow! Top attraction, I'd say.'

'Well, sorry to pour cold water on your idea, but, as I've explained, these guns don't actually spray. Your target has to be just underneath the nozzle. Can you imagine your mates hanging around underneath a giant-sized gun, waiting to be coated with icing sugar?'

'Sounds rather d-delicious to me,' said Stringfellow as he settled down at the kitchen table. 'Bit like being under a sh-sherbet fountain.'

'It's the shooting part that's the fun, Stringfellow. You know, covering everybody with icing sugar.'

'Hey, if that won't work, say we do the same thing with water guns at the Big BuzZ? You know – the really massive ones.'

'Brilliantissimo!'

'Yes, great for my field too,' said Gramps. 'An afternoon with masses of children doing that and you'd turn it into a swamp.'

'Okay, I've got an even better idea. Instead of the children squirting water at each other, why can't they have an adult target? And he'd be the one with the massive water gun and the children would pelt him with wet sponges.'

'Well, now you're talking.'

'Got the idea from our school fête,' said Ben. They charged fifty pence for a bucket of five sponges to lob at the headmaster and it was by far the most popular stand. So,' he continued, looking at the adults, 'any volunteers?'

'Well, I've got a suggestion,' said Chris, pouring tea as he spoke. 'The adult carrying the water gun could be very tall and dressed in a long black robe with a hood – like the grim reaper.'

'Who's the grim reaper?'

'It used to be a way of describing death. He was portrayed as a black hooded figure carrying a scythe – except of course our grim reaper would be carrying a water gun.'

'You're a genius, Chris,' exclaimed Ben. 'So this grim reaper with the gun, he'd be pretending to spray glyphosates?'

'Wicked. And are you thinking what I'm thinking, Chris?' Rory broke in excitedly. 'Barty'd be perfect if he'd do it, don't you think, Seb?'

'Bartholomew Broadbum – is he the guy who looks like a beanpole?'

'The very one, Ben, and his name is Bartholomew Broadbeam. Might be a good idea to get that right if you intend to ask him.'

'Cool. And I've had another idea. Once when we were on holiday we went to a medieval day at a castle and they had all sorts of great games that people actually played in the Middle Ages. One of them was super cool. You're trying to balance on a log and you've got to try and swing this great sack of straw so that it knocks your opponent off theirs.'

'I've an idea,' said Gramps. 'How about in our version there's one adult in the middle of the ring and all the youngsters take turns in swinging the sack to knock him down.'

'Don't tell me, Toby,' Seb broke in. This adult is going to be very large – what you'd call a "Big Boy", I daresay. And the kids are all going to be ganging up to knock him off.

Empowering the People, eh? Had someone particular in mind, by any chance?'

Rory started to giggle. 'Oh, come on, Stringfellow. You'd be a brilliant target.'

'What! Stand there all afternoon representing the evils of agrochemicals while a load of kids take turns socking me with sacks of hay? I'll just keep to the demonstration, thank you very much.'

'Oh please, Stringfellow! We'd want to give you a break so we'll find one or two other volunteers to do it too.'

'Great idea,' said Ben enthusiastically. 'And how about this? All the big boys could wear special T-shirts saying Big Oil, Big Tobacco and, what was the one you just said, Stringfellow? Agrochemicals?'

Surprisingly, it was Rory not Gramps who answered.

'The companies who make pesticides, you noodle. Great idea about the T-shirts, though.'

Stringfellow's expression was suddenly serious. 'Speaking of neonics, Ben, I've been thinking some more about what you t-told us this morning about the three bees who were dying. You said that the one who actually died warned you about oilseed rape, remember? Well, neonicotinoids have often been used on oilseed rape.'

Gramps and Chris were both open-mouthed as they looked at Stringfellow. He seemed not only to have taken Ben's dream very seriously, but had remembered every detail.

Stringfellow continued. 'Didn't she s-say something about beware hogwood?'

Rory started giggling. 'Hogwart, don't you mean? You're not suggesting that the bees know about Harry Potter, are you, Stringfellow?'

'No, you cheeky madam. I'm suggesting that Ben thought he heard her say "Ogwood", but what he actually heard was "hogweed". That could be very exciting. And something else, Ben,' he continued. 'Didn't you say the bee who died had said something like "beware the Oppies". The name rang a bell with me. It so happens I've a friend, a Professor at Sussex University, who has been doing some very interesting research. Dave Goulson is his name and he's world renowned for his work on bees. If Chris will let you use his computer, I think you'll find something on his website that will help your investigation. Worth a t-try anyway.'

Five minutes later Ben and Rory were up in what Chris called his office. It was actually a cubbyhole at the top of the stairs next to his bedroom. Luckily Chris had all his papers tidily in files and the desk was clear for Ben to get out his notebook, turn on the computer and google the name of Stringfellow's friend – and then the word "hogweed".

Ben and Rory were open-mouthed at what this combination produced. *Research exposes secret cocktail of toxic pesticides in hedgerows*, they saw.

Then, in a puzzled voice, Ben started reading aloud the list that followed, '*Creeping buttercup, scented mayweed, burnet saxifrage, fool's parsley* . . .' What? It sounded like a load of old weeds.

Disappointed and impatient, he jumped to the end of the list – then leapt out of his chair in excitement.

'Rory, look! Hogweed and poppy! Not "Beware Oppies" – "Beware poppies!" That's what the dying bee was saying.'

Delighted, they stared at each other, then carried on reading.

'Wow, Rory, we're really on to something now. It seems like lots of people already know that neonics are dangerous for bees – and other wildlife. But now it looks as if the problem is way, way bigger than that.'

Ben had his notebook ready and was beginning to copy out: *Scientists have discovered that bees are exposed to a chemical cocktail when feeding from wildflowers next to neonicotinoid treated crops…*when he stopped, puzzled.

He looked at Rory. 'You seem to know a bit about fertilisers. Any idea what these cocktails are?'

Rory didn't answer, but disappeared off to her bedroom and came back with a folder in her hand. She looked at the sentence Ben was busily copying: *In addition to neonicotinoids, farmers may spray some non-organic crops a dozen or more times while they are growing with anything up to twenty-three different chemicals.*

'That's it, you see, Ben. It's the mixture of the different chemicals – fertilisers, pesticides, whatever – that make the cocktail.' She held out the folder. 'Look at what I did for a project in Geography. I made it into a story, but all the facts in it are absolutely true. Do you want to read it?'

Ben looked at the folder, which was decorated with a picture of a tree. 'It's beautiful. Did you do the drawing too?'

'It's not very good really.'

'It's wicked. I think you should read the story to all of us. If it's something to do with these chemical cocktails, well, your pal Stringfellow is bound to be interested.' He paused, then said, 'Listen, Rory, before we go down to them, I wanted to ask you something. I keep thinking about what might be going on at Broadacres. Let's face it, you might like Mr Corbridge, but he does own a massive amount of land – all within the reach of Gramps's bees and Gramps has lost practically all of them.'

He looked to see what effect his words were having on Rory, but her stony face gave nothing away. He guessed she was thinking how awkward it would be for her if it should turn out to be true that Vanessa's dad was using neonics and possibly other dangerous chemicals too. It wouldn't do her friendship with Vanessa much good, that was for sure.

'I've really got to help Gramps,' he said urgently. 'And we want to be sure the surviving bees aren't killed as well, don't we? Think of Frontoback and Wonky, Rory.'

Rory still didn't reply.

'Look, if you don't believe Vanessa's dad could be using neonicotinoids, why don't I go up there secretly and have a look? Then I wouldn't be accusing him of something without any proof.'

'Oh yes, Mr Private Investigator. I suppose you're just going to wander around on private property hoping to come across the place where he keeps his nics – if he's got any. It's a massive place. There's loads of barns.'

'I sort of thought you might have some idea. You could make me a little map maybe?' He looked at Rory pleadingly.

'You're daft. I've told you, it's massive there. The only thing I could do is find out where the spraying machines are when I go riding with Vanessa. I mean, whatever sprays he's using are pretty likely to be stored nearby.'

'You're a sport, Rory.' He paused, but only for a moment. 'So when are you going riding with Vanessa, then?'

'Well, luckily for you, early tomorrow morning. Shall we go down to the others now?' Rory picked up her book.

The three men were still chatting at the table, mugs of coffee in their hands.

'You've been a while,' said Stringfellow. 'Any use, that website?'

'Brilliant!' Ben's face had a huge grin. 'Fantastic lead. Thanks so much, Stringfellow.'

'So, are you letting us in on the secret?' asked Chris.

'Yes,' said Ben, waving a piece of paper. 'It's not a secret anyway. This article explains exactly why neonicotinoids are so deadly. You've got to read it. The problem is that, as you know, farmers spray all sorts of other chemicals as well. So, even when they think they're spraying crops which bees aren't interested in, they're contaminating the wildflowers in hedgerows nearby where the bees love foraging . . .' He paused, then announced in a slow emphatic voice, 'And so the neonicotinoids become part of a deadly chemical cocktail.'

He watched with satisfaction as Gramps's eyebrows shot up and Chris's jaw dropped.

'Good heavens!' Gramps banged his coffee back on the table so forcefully that its contents splashed everywhere.

'Steady on, Toby,' murmured Chris as he wiped some from his face. He went off to fetch a cloth.

Gramps seemed not have noticed and carried on, 'But this is shocking news, Ben. Explain a bit more about these chemical cocktails will you?'

'I can do better than that,' said Ben grandly. 'I now have the pleasure of introducing my colleague, Miss Aurora Cremona, who will read to us from her latest research on chemical cocktails.'

Rory's normally pale cheeks flushed pink. 'Stop being such a stupid twit, Ben. It isn't my research. And it's a story.'

'A very interesting one it sounds like. Come sit down and read it to us. We're all ears,' said Stringfellow.

THE STORY OF NEEM

Once upon a time – but not so very long ago – a young girl called Neha was growing up in a little village in India. She had dark shiny eyes, long straight hair and a merry laugh. No. That is not quite true. When she was a little girl, she had laughed a lot, but there was no longer much to laugh about in the village.

The village she lived in was called Punukula and it was in the state of Andhra Pradesh. Neha's father was a farmer. He didn't have a lot of land and they didn't have a lot of money, but they always had enough to eat and the family – for Neha had an older brother, Nila – were happy as larks.

But one day, when Neha was still very small, some strange men came to the village. 'We have good news for you,' they said. 'Call everyone together tonight and we will tell you all about it.'

That evening when the villagers were seated on the ground the taller of the two men began to speak.

'You are very lucky, my friends. I have brought you cotton seeds at such a very reasonable price. You will be able to grow the most wonderful cotton from them, and you will earn a lot of money from your crop. And not only this. I have fertilisers and pesticides to go with the seed so you will have very large crops and you will not be troubled by horrible pests.

'And what is m o r e,' he said, stretching out the more and then repeating it, 'what is m o r e, 'if you haven't any money now, no problem. Because I represent a very rich, foreign company you don't need to pay until the crop is harvested and ready for sale. So come, my friends. Take advantage.'

The villagers looked at each other in disbelief. It was truly a wonderful offer. They didn't need to pay any money straight away – which was just as well, for the farmers had very little. They only needed to pay when the crop was ready and the two men promised that they would buy all that the villagers could produce. How could they lose?

And, indeed, all happened as the men had promised. And these were happy years in the village. Neha was now old enough to go to the fields by herself and she proudly took her father his lunch in a basket and sat with him while he ate.

'Daughter, we are so lucky,' he would say. 'Never have I grown such an abundant crop. And I need to use so little of the fertiliser the men sold us.'

'How wonderful, father,' said Neha. 'But what is "furtiliza"?'

'Oh, it is a magical thing. When you put it on the soil, you can grow more cotton and better cotton.'

Neha's eyes grew bigger at the thought of this magic "furtiliza".

But soon the problems began. The cotton took a lot of goodness from the soil and the fertilisers did nothing to replace it – even though the farmers used more and more.

Worse was to come. To begin with there had been no pests. But very soon horrible cotton pests like bellworms and aphids arrived and began to feed on the cotton. The farmers were not too worried. They simply applied the insecticides they had bought on credit. They thought these would certainly kill all the pests. But they only destroyed the weaker ones. The stronger ones became even stronger – they became, in fact, resistant. So though the farmers were using more and more pesticide no amount of these chemicals could kill the bugs.

Worse, the farmers did not realise that, without meaning to, they had been killing other wildlife – birds, beetles, spiders and other predators – which normally would have eaten the cotton pests.

In their desperation, when the villagers saw that using more pesticides was not working, they began to mix them together. They did not realise that the chemicals became even more dangerous when mixed up. And that the evil potion they created, and which they sprayed on the crops as often as twice a week, were named a 'chemical cocktail' by scientists. Nor did they realize that scientists had warned people to be careful, for these cocktails were not only dangerous to wildlife but to humans too!

Gone were the happy times in the village. The farmers were now badly in debt. The crops they grew were never large enough for them to be able to pay back the multinational company for all the chemicals they were using. Before, though they'd never had much money, they'd always had enough to eat. Now they were often hungry.

Neha's family had never been rich. But Neha's father always made sure there were sacks of rice put aside in case harvests were not good. There were families in the village who were far poorer than them.

Neha worried about her friend Ansuya. She had become so thin. When they went to school Neha always shared her lunch with her. One day when she met her as usual so they could walk to school together Ansuya was crying. Her father had warned her that, as there wasn't enough food left for all the family and she was a girl, and the eldest girl in the family, he might have to send her away to work.

Neha tried to comfort her friend. 'He is so kind your father. He will never do that.' But she continued to worry. She knew that there were children who had been sold to rich farmers as indentured labour and they had not been seen again in the village.

She tried to speak to her father about it, but her father had developed a mysterious rash on his skin. Since it had begun to spread all over his body he had become very irritable and had no patience to listen to Neha.

'Ansuya's family are at least healthy. They are lucky.

Look at your brother – he is always tired, feeling sick, having headaches. Don't you think I have enough to worry about?'

Then Neha felt very guilty. She knew her father depended on Noni's help. And she guessed he was frightened that this was only the beginning, There were people in the village who'd become seriously ill. They had mysterious nerve problems or problems with their sight. And there was no money for them to see doctors.

'We never had these problems before we used the "cocktails",' the villagers said.

So Neha kept her worries to herself now. But one day when it was time for the long walk to school Ansuya was not at their usual meeting place. She had never missed school before.

Neha found the day very long. She couldn't wait to get out of school to go and find out if Ansuya was sick too. When she arrived at their hut, she found Ansuya's mother wailing outside. She cried out when she saw Neha.

'She's not here, Neha. Her father's taken her and she's gone.' She didn't need to explain. Neha ran to her and they sobbed together.

But her tears were not finished. At night when her family were asleep she wept for her friend again and this continued for many weeks. Would she ever see Ansuya again?

Some weeks later there was news in the village. A man and a woman had arrived and wanted to speak to all the villagers. The villagers were very suspicious.

'Not more people wanting to sell us things,' they said.

However, they were curious and that night gathered round to listen to the strangers. The woman stood up to speak.

'Friends, my name is Prishila and this is Rajesh.' She pointed at the man. 'We come to you from Secure.' There was whispering among the villagers.

'Secure,' they said. 'Oh yes. This is surely another of those big foreign companies. But we will not be tricked again.'

The two strangers heard the muttering. 'We do not come from a multinational,' said Prishila. 'Secure is an organisation that can advise you how to overcome the very problems which the chemicals sold by such companies have caused you. We do not want to sell you anything. The remedy we suggest is quite free.'

Now the villagers were beginning to look interested and sat quietly, waiting to hear more.

When Prishila saw she had their attention, she began to talk about a wonderful tree: 'So wonderful,' she said, 'that it seems to have magic powers.'

'The neem tree,' she said, 'has its own defences to protect itself from pest insects. What it does is produce substances that discourage pest insects from laying eggs, substances that interfere with their growth and, perhaps most important of all, substances that make it more difficult for them to sense their food – and so the pests starve.

And because the neem tree produces such a variety of

chemicals, the tree's insect enemies can't grow resistant to them.'

This sounded extremely interesting.

'But maybe best of all,' she continued, 'unlike the pesticides that the chemical company sold you, neem toxins are harmless to humans and to other wildlife and insects. Only the pest insects die.'

'How do we use these things that the neem tree produces?' asked Neha's father.

'Let me show you,' said Prishila, and she brought out some powder in a bag and a solid lump of something she called neem cake.

* * *

Then she explained how the villagers could make their own powder by grinding neem leaves and seeds and then soaking the powder overnight. Then it was ready to be sprayed on the crops.

'Now this is just one small piece of neem cake,' she said, holding it up in her hand. 'What you do with neem cake is crumble it up and mix it into the soil. This wonderful cake not only kills pests and diseases in the soil but works as a fertiliser, so the soil is enriched.

'And when can you give us some?' the villagers asked in great excitement.

'Why, you have plenty of neem trees growing nearby. You only have to gather the leaves and grind them. You will have nothing to pay for these wonderful products,' said Prishila.

Now the villagers looked less sure. Like most people, they were frightened of change. And what if they spent their time grinding the leaves and it didn't work?

But Neha's father was thinking about his son. When he and his wife had taken him to the local hospital they had been told that their son was desperately ill with pesticide poisoning (which they could see perfectly well for themselves) and that only very expensive treatment in hospital (which they couldn't possibly afford) would help him. So Neha's father was prepared to do anything that might help him and he volunteered to try out the natural methods.

Neha and her mother were very excited too. 'I will help you with the grinding, Father,' said Neha, and they began to gather the leaves straight away. She began to spend all her spare time when she wasn't at school grinding away.

When the villagers weren't working in their fields, they came to watch Neha. 'It's such a lot of work all that grinding and who knows what will happen,' they said.

Meanwhile Prishila came back to visit them and showed them how to discover when the crops were full of bollworms. That way they only had to spray neem when the bollworms were abundant.

Some of the villagers were curious about what Neha's family were doing – but many just scoffed.

'You really think you can protect your crop by spraying this neem powder a few times when we put on expensive commercial pesticide twice a week and it doesn't work?

Huh!' they sneered. 'You simple fellow, believing all this talk of magic.'

But, as the time of the cotton harvest came near, they stopped scoffing. Neha's father's crop was every bit as good as theirs and all the profit was his own. Better still, Noni began to recover his strength.

They now had enough to eat and Neha's father could even save money from what he had earned for their cotton. Neha's cheeks grew fuller and she even began to smile again.

But she wasn't quite the old Neha with the merry laugh. She couldn't forget the fate of Ansuya, toiling unpaid for some farmer far away. A farmer she couldn't run away from however mean he might be to her because she had to stay and pay off her father's debt.

Meanwhile the women in the village noticed how Noni, who had been so seriously ill, was now strong enough to help his father again. They thought of their own families. Many had husbands who had got ill – or even died.

Just as bad, because the villagers had no money for expensive machinery, they sprayed the chemicals by hand with small sprays. And the children helped. But, of course, the small sprays meant they were very close to the dangerous pesticides. And so many children got sick as well.

'Look how much better Noni is,' they said to their husbands. 'You can see that what the people from Secure said is true. This neem is not trickery – it is real magic. We should use it too.'

Little by little they managed to convince their husbands and gradually the villagers' health improved and their farms became profitable again. Punakula was once again a happy village.

But Neha had not forgotten Ansuya.

One day she said to her father, 'Now that we have money saved, can we use some of it to loan money to Ansuya's father? Then he will be able to pay off his debt to the farmer that Ansuya is working for.'

Neha's father agreed. Neha had been such a great help to him; he was proud of her and he wanted to hear her laugh again.

So Ansuya came back to the village and the girls fell into each other's arms. 'You are much taller now, but so very bony,' said Neha as they hugged. Ansuya's mother had prepared a special meal for her daughter and she ate eagerly and kept refilling her plate for she had not had so much to eat and certainly nothing so tasty for a great while.

Neha asked if she would be coming back to school. 'How can I?' said Ansuya sadly. 'I have missed so much. I can never catch up with you.'

'If I help you, though, you will be able to.' And it was true. Having worked long hours in the fields, Ansuya was so happy to go back to school and study that it wasn't too long before she had caught up.

Maybe you think this is the happy ending of the story – but it isn't actually a story. Everything is true and so there isn't an ending! The story of Neem, the magic tree, is continuing.

Neha and Ansuya's schooldays are over now. Their village was becoming a very different place even while they were still at school – more healthy and more prosperous. The villagers were able to rescue all the indentured children, some of whom who had been away for many years. The village organised special classes for them so that they could catch up with their classmates who had remained in school.

And Neha and Ansuya had been hatching plans together. As soon as they left school, they set up a project for collecting, grinding and selling neem to other villages. This went so well that many women in the village joined them. Their project became a real business.

Prishila and Rajesh were very impressed with what these two girls had achieved.

They were invited to come to work at Secure and join the team of people taking the story of neem to other villages.

Already by 2008, three thousand villages in the region of Panukula were using neem. The escape from pesticide addiction is continuing to spread.

Chapter Seventeen

There was complete silence when Rory finished reading. She looked up to see that Chris was nodding, and Stringfellow and Gramps were shaking their heads.

'What's up?' she said.

Ben answered for them. 'I think they're just amazed.'

'Spot on,' agreed Gramps.

'Fascinating piece of work, young lady,' exclaimed Stringfellow. 'I thought I was a bit of an expert on growing organically and avoiding using pesticides, but I never realised quite how dangerous some of these chemicals and fertilisers can be to human health.'

'Is everything in your story absolutely true?' asked Chris.

'Well, everything except the names of the characters. And Neha and Ansuya are made up. But all the things that happened to them did happen there. Still are happening, actually.'

'It's an inspiring story, Rory. Very impressive. Lots of interesting implications for this country too.' He turned to Stringfellow. 'You probably picked up that the province of Andhra Pradesh is supporting farmers who use organic methods.'

'I did,' said Stringfellow. 'Let's hope that we get a more enlightened government in this country one of these days.'

'Hoping won't get us very far, Stringfellow. It all depends on us! All aboard for the demo, I say!' Ben leapt up, making fists with his hands and punching the air around him energetically.

'Whoops! Keep out of his way or he'll land you one, Seb,' warned Chris. 'Dangerous, these Busbys, when they get excited.'

Chapter Eighteen

The next day, Ben watched the sugar crystals dissolve in the water. The saucepan was on a gentle flame.

'Watch out. Don't overheat it,' Gramps warned. 'It's sugar syrup we're after, not burnt toffee!'

'Okay, okay.' Ben was savouring the sweet scent of the melting sugar. It reminded him of the caramel sauce he made with Mum and put on sliced oranges. He licked his lips at the thought.

It had been his idea to make the sugar syrup for the bees. Gramps made a fudgy sort of fondant, which Ben called bee toffee, to give to the bees in winter. Occasionally, though, in the spring he fed them with sugar syrup when a long period of rainy weather had kept them in the hive. Well, if ever emergency measures were called for it was now.

'Frontoback and Wonky were pretty hungry, Gramps. I bet Bustlealong was too – she never stopped for a snack, though. And none of them were eating as much as they wanted because they were thinking of all the other bees that needed to eat as well. I wish I knew which hive they're in, Gramps. But I'm sure all the colonies would be happy to have a tray of sugar syrup – rain or no rain.'

'I think you're right, Ben. And it so happens I've stocked up on sugar. We can do it this morning.' Now they had six plastic canisters filled with the sugar syrup.

'Let's have a break for lunch and then maybe you'd like to help me fill the trays. Toasted-cheese sandwiches sound good?'

'Very,' said Ben, but what he was really thinking was that it was already lunchtime and not a word from Rory. She'd promised to phone as soon as she'd got back from riding, and for the last hour even the syrup-making hadn't distracted him.

The sandwiches appeared and disappeared. Still no sound from Ben's mobile.

'Are you sure you want to help me with the trays, Ben? You've been very busy this morning with all that syrup.'

'Quite sure, Gramps,' he said, thinking he needed some distraction anyway.

He stuck his mobile in his pocket and helped Gramps fill two boxes with the sugar-syrup canisters. They carried the boxes to the hives and began filling the trays Gramps had put inside with the syrup.

'That Rory has a real gift for storytelling, hasn't she, Ben?'

'She's really good,' agreed Ben.

'Fascinating story,' he continued, 'and what an inspiring ending. I think we should make a little book for her, get it printed and sell it at the Big BuzZ.'

'Wicked idea, Gramps. And she's done some drawings, too, while she's been here. She's shy about them, but I think they're great.'

'Well, see what she thinks, then. That's her coming down the path now.'

Ben looked up eagerly.

'What are you two doing? Can I help?'

Ben frowned at her. He needed to speak to her privately. Too late for that now. Gramps was already explaining what they'd been doing and Rory was eager to fill a tray herself. It was what seemed like half an hour before he could get her away from Gramps and the hives.

'What took you so long? You promised to call me when you got back.' They were walking back to the house. Ben had offered to make a mug of tea for Gramps.

'Couldn't help it. Vanessa asked me to stay for lunch. Couldn't exactly say, "Love to, but first I've got to give some information to a private investigator I'm helping," could I?'

'Suppose not. But have you got the information, then?'

'What do you want first – the good news or the bad news?'

'Whatever.'

'Well, I did manage to find out which barn has all the spraying machinery and stuff.' She paused and looked at Ben. They were back in the house and he was filling the kettle.

'You might like to say thank you. It wasn't exactly easy pretending to Vanessa that I was suddenly so interested in farm machinery.'

'Sorry, Rory. Thanks very much. I really am grateful. So what's the bad news?'

'Problem is that the barns are much too close to the house and the stables and everything. I mean, you can't just go poking around there without attracting someone's attention. I was hoping the stuff you're interested in would be in a field somewhere away from the other buildings. Here. I've made you a little map, but I don't think it's going to be any use to you.'

Ben looked at it and then thought for a minute. 'Well, who said I was intending to go during the day? Much safer in the dark.' He hadn't really made any plan at all, but, now he started to think about it, it would be safer – and more fun – to go at night.

'You're crazy. You've never even been inside the estate. How are you going to find your way around in the dark? And they might have vicious guard dogs.'

'Do they?'

'Well, they have signs on their gates saying beware of guard dogs. They don't start with me 'cos I'm with Vanessa. But who knows what they'd do if they thought you were breaking in.'

She paused and sighed. 'Suppose I'm going to have to come with you, aren't I?'

'Here, Rory.' Ben proffered a toothbrush. 'I've found you a new one.'

Rory was sitting on Ben's bed in a pair of his pyjamas. They'd decided that they should take advantage of the full moon to go and explore at Broadacres that night. Gramps had agreed to their sudden plan that Rory should sleep over 'to discuss what needed to be done to organise the Big BuzZ'.

They'd made a roasted-vegetable lasagne for supper. By the time they'd prepared it and eaten it, they'd planned all their publicity, decided how and where they'd distribute the flyers, which newspapers they'd speak to and who else they'd ask to take part.

Ben had his mouth full of particularly luscious strawberry ice cream.

When was the last time I ate one as good as this? he wondered as he helped himself to some more. Then it came to him.

'The place we stayed in France – you know where we did all those games? – well, one night they had this organic fair thing. People made all kinds of delicious stuff and sold it. There were sausages, beef burgers, pancakes, waffles and ice cream made with organic fruit . . .'

'Okay, got the message. You had a major pig-out!'

'But listen. There was all the stuff that adults like to buy as well. You know, bread, cheese, quiches, wine, beer. And trestle tables for people to sit and scoff it so it was like a party.' He looked at Gramps. 'Are there a lot of people growing organic food round here, do you think?'

'Certainly are. But you'd best ask your friend Stringfellow. He's bound to know all the local producers. Suggesting that we combine the Big Buzz with a sort of organic fête, are you?'

'Why not if it brings people in? I mean people do like to go places where there's masses of things to eat and loads of things to amuse their children, don't they? And the local producers would get to sell their stuff to zillions of new customers.'

'Zillions, eh? I suggest you two get some sleep now with all you've got planned for tomorrow and we talk about it some more in the morning.'

He was surprised that this was all it took for them to vanish upstairs.

'I thought we'd put the alarm on for one o'clock.' Ben fiddled with his mobile. 'Everyone will be bound to be asleep then, don't you think, Rory?'

Chapter Nineteen

Just as Ben had hoped, a large moon was overhead as they crept out of the back door.

They'd borrowed two big torches from Gramps. (Maybe 'borrowed' wasn't quite the right word as they hadn't actually asked him, thought Ben. But what reason could they invent for suddenly needing them that night?)

For the moment, though, the torches were unnecessary. They could see quite clearly in the silvery light. Ben put them in his saddlebag for later.

They walked the bikes quietly over the grass until they were sure they were out of earshot.

Then they got on their bikes, pedalled towards the gate and turned into the lane.

Ben was in a fizz of excitement. Finding out stuff on the internet had been interesting, but real-life investigation was way more exciting. And investigating in the moonlight . . .

A wide grin spread over his face, which he hoped Rory couldn't see.

But Rory was looking in wonder at the shadows they were casting on the path as they cycled along, and the shadows of the trees, shifting slightly as their branches moved in the breeze. In the magic of the moonlight, her fears about helping Ben to snoop around the Corbridge's property were almost forgotten.

The magic lost its effect, however, when, fifteen minutes later, they arrived at the entrance to Broadacres. There was no gate to prevent them entering, but, as she'd warned Ben, there was a sign warning them to BEWARE OF THE DOGS on one of the gateposts.

They paused a moment.

'Where are they, then?' asked Ben, looking around. He felt himself shivering as he heard a rustling in the hedgerow and saw a movement of leaves.

'How big are they?' he whispered when Rory didn't answer. He wished he'd thought of bringing biscuits or something to give them.

'They're very big and very black and, if you didn't know them, they'd be very scary. Especially when they open their dribbly mouths and you see their big teeth and lolling tongues and hear them panting.'

Ben's eyes grew large. He stared at her to see if she was having him on.

'But they'll recognise you, won't they?' he asked.

'Hope so,' said Rory. 'Anyway, most likely the sign is only there to scare off burglars. The dogs haven't turned up so probably they're asleep in the house.'

'How far is it to the house?'

'We're not going to the house, are we? We go up the drive here then we turn off on a path to the right and that's where all the barns and the stables are.'

'Okay, party leader. I think we can risk cycling up. Won't be anyone around at this time.'

In the silvery light it was quite easy to see the buildings – a whole cluster of them.

'I'd never have known where to start.' He spoke in a low voice. It seemed part of the adventure that they should be whispering even though there were no humans around.

'That's the one.' She pointed at a great big oblong metal building.

'But that's not a barn, surely. It looks more like a warehouse or something. It's massive.'

'Thinking of the pretty barns you see in picture books? With little chickens and ducklings clucking around them. Well, I suppose you can't help being a towny. Most farms are big business now so they've got their very large and expensive tractors and machinery safely locked up in—'

Ben interrupted before she'd finished her sentence.

'You didn't say anything about locks.'

'I meant they're shut up, but . . .' She looked worried. 'Those big doors were open when we came past this morning. They may not be locked.'

They propped their bikes against the side of the barn and went to the front to have a look.

There was no need to try to open the big doors. A big padlock was attached to the lock.

They stood a moment, looking in silence. All Ben's excitement had drained out of him.

'Suppose that's it. Can't start breaking in,' he said flatly. 'Except . . . could there be another way in? I mean, if they're

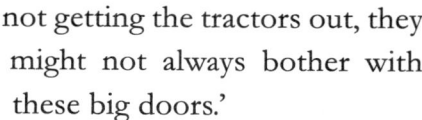

not getting the tractors out, they might not always bother with these big doors.'

'Good thinking, super sleuth. Let's have a look around.'

They turned round the side of the building. Sure enough, in the wall halfway down, was a doorway.

'Probably locked too.'

'Doubt it,' said Rory. 'You can't get a tractor out that way. It's all the expensive machinery they're trying to protect. I'm going to try.'

She turned the handle and the door opened easily.

'Right. Here we go.' Compared to the moonlit outside, the barn was pitch black. As their eyes adjusted, Ben shone his torch around. Strange shapes loomed in the dark. Large machines Ben had never seen before.

'What are they? They look like mechanical monsters.'

'That's what sprayers look like when they're folded back like wings.'

'Well, we're in the right place, then. Let the search commence!'

The light of their torches swung around the walls. The beams soon found rows of what looked like giant tins.

'What are those?' said Ben. He was already speeding across the barn.

'Could be just what you're looking for.'

Their torchlight found the labels on the immense canisters.

'See that, Rory? clothianidin,' said Ben triumphantly. 'Just what we suspected!'

'Did we? I've never heard of it.'

'Well, I have. One of the most common kinds of neonicotinoids,' he announced authoritatively. 'Now let's see what else we can find here.' Their torch beams continued to travel over the canisters' labels.

Suddenly Ben turned to Rory 'Look, that's Chloro-thal-Chlorothalonil!!! Wow what a tongue twister. Whoever thinks of these names.'

'What about it, then?'

'I recognise that name from when I was looking up chemical cocktails yesterday. I'm sure it was one of those on that website Stringfellow told me about. If you use it at the same time as neonics it makes them much, much more dangerous for bees. This is the proof we needed Rory. This is why so many of Gramps's bees have died or disappeared.' He turned to Rory, grinning widely, but she looked far from happy. 'What is it, Rory?'

'I don't know, Ben. I suppose I was sort of hoping that we wouldn't find anything here – anything that proves Mr Corbridge is using this stuff, I mean. Now what do I do when you go accusing Vanessa's father?'

The grin had slipped off Ben's face too, and all his excitement at their discovery vanished. He should never have let Rory get involved, he realised. But he'd carry on without her help.

'Don't worry, Rory. I understand and no one has to know you were with me. I shan't let on. And I've got all the proof

I need. Shall we go home now?' He looked down at her where she was crouching among the canisters.

Before she could answer there was a slight sound behind them. They turned their heads towards the door. Suddenly they were dazzled by strong lights. All the fluorescent lights in the barn had come on.

Then a harsh voice called out, 'What the hell is going on in here?'

A tall man in a dressing gown was standing by the door, looking around. His face was puffed up and red with anger, and his eyes were bulging unpleasantly like the eyes of a bull terrier. Two black dogs were panting eagerly at his feet. Ben's heart was pounding. Those dogs would find them any second.

'Don't move,' he whispered to Rory. His legs had become water, but he forced himself to step out from among the canisters.

His stomach was churning. He tried to speak. 'I . . . I . . .' His tongue had become a useless lump in his mouth.

'You . . . you . . . what exactly?' sneered Mr Corbridge.

'I-I was just looking to see—'

'Oh. Just looking to see, were you? The alarm wakes us all at two a.m. because you were just looking to see. That it?'

'Alarm?' repeated Ben, feeling stupid as the word slipped out.

'That's right, alarm. While you were busy *looking*, the alarm went off at the house. Not heard of alarms? Or perhaps you thought that, if there was one, it would have rung here and warned you to scarper?'

'I . . . I . . .' Ben's tongue still couldn't produce any words.

'And you needed an accomplice for your "looking", did you?' Mr Corbridge's fierce gaze was fixed meaningfully on Ben's face.

Ben felt his stomach sinking further. He'd never got himself into a worse mess – or rather he'd never got someone else into such a mess. Being discovered had been scary enough, but the possibility that Rory would be found was wringing his insides out. How could he possibly get her out undetected?

'Accomplice?' he asked weakly, to gain time.

'Can you speak, boy, or do you just echo? Yes, ac-com-plice. Do you understand that word? Where is your partner in crime?'

'No, no, really, it was just me who thought of investigating.' In the need to protect Rory, Ben had suddenly found his voice. He started to walk towards Mr Corbridge to distract his gaze from Rory's hiding place.

'Indeed. So how do you explain the two bikes outside? I believe I've seen the purple one before. Rather unusual, purple bikes.' There was a grim smile of triumph on Mr Corbridge's face.

A feeling of sick fear came over Ben. There seemed no way now to protect Rory.

It seemed she, too, had decided there was no way out for there was a slight scuffling sound from behind the canisters and she stood up. Ben couldn't bear to look at her face, tight with misery.

'I'm so sorry, Mr Corbridge. We were just investigating. It's some . . .' Her voice faltered. It wasn't her normal voice. It was the kind of voice that comes just before tears.

'It's some research we've been doing – about how mixtures of different pesticides and fungicides can be deadly to wildlife – and possibly to humans too. And Ben's grandpa, who is one of your neighbours, has lost most of his bees.'

'I'm afraid I still don't understand, Rory.' Mr Corbridge's grim face was turned to her now and his voice was clipped and cold. 'Why exactly did you think you needed to investigate in the middle of the night? Couldn't you have come to speak to me in the daytime?'

Because you would have denied it, thought Ben, but neither he nor Rory answered.

Mr Corbridge broke the silence. 'Well, you've woken my whole household setting the alarm off. I think I'd better get back to the house and reassure them that it wasn't burglars but two youngsters who broke in –' he paused – 'and that one of them was Rory.'

Ben and Rory were now standing side by side and Ben didn't need to look at her to feel her misery.

'Get off home now before anyone has a chance to find that you've gone and start worrying.' He looked at Ben. 'I'll be over to speak to your grandpa tomorrow.'

There were few words spoken on the way home. Ben had tried to apologise to Rory for getting her involved, but got no answer. He tried reassuring her that Vanessa wouldn't necessarily blame her for the break-in.

But all his attempts to make her feel better met with a stony silence. He gave up trying. The only words he could get out of her were, 'I'm going back to Chris's for the rest of the night.' In silence they pedalled over to Timbertops. Rory managed a cool, "Night, then,' and in black misery Ben turned round and rode back to Gramps's house.

Chapter Twenty

'I don't know what you were thinking about, Ben. Of all the hare-brained ideas. Frankly, you're lucky he didn't call the police.'

'The police? We were just looking.'

'Police, Ben. Breaking and entering. That mean anything to you? You were very lucky he didn't call them as soon as the alarm went off. Quite foolhardy of him, in fact, to go out to the barn by himself. The kind of people who go breaking into barns intending to steal valuable machinery could quite easily be violent as well.'

'But, Gramps, I just wanted to get proof before we spoke to him. I mean he could just have denied that he uses all that stuff, couldn't he?'

'That's all very well, Ben. You've got your proof now and what exactly are you going to do about it? Not exactly in a position to have a friendly chat and try to persuade him to stop using them for the sake of my bees, are you?'

Friendly chat? Ben hadn't even got as far as warning Gramps

that Mr Corbridge would be coming round to have a very unfriendly chat – possibly any moment.

'I'm sorry, Gramps, but I had to do something for the bees . . .' He felt tears pricking his eyes and hoped Gramps hadn't noticed. 'I never imagined it would all . . . all go so wrong. And it's worse than you think.' He was blinking hard – fighting with the tears that were still threatening to fall. 'Rory's gone home,' he finished.

'I'd realised that.'

'Yes, but she's not talking to me now. *She* never thought it was a good idea. She was just helping me.'

'Well, I can see you've put her in a very embarrassing position.' Gramps paused. His eyebrows were meeting bushily over his nose, but he looked more thoughtful than angry. He looked at Ben's cereal. Ben had been pushing it around his bowl for the last five minutes and it was an unappealing mush

'Why don't you try to eat some of that cereal? No, better still, take some fresh. Then I'll take you round to the Corbridges'. You can apologise and explain that it wasn't Rory's plan. Might help.'

'Thanks, Gramps.' He managed to sound grateful, but the thought of meeting Mr Corbridge again turned his guts back to water and made him quite unable to swallow the fresh cereal with which Gramps had refilled his bowl.

The daylight trip to Broadacres was very different to the excitement of the moonlit cycle ride of the night before. All too soon they were driving through the gateposts and on to the drive that led to the house. It was empty of cars or any other sign of life.

They walked up the wide steps that led to the house and Gramps rang the front doorbell, a big brass one that clanged loudly.

Think positive, Ben told himself. He pulled himself up to his full height and tried to hide his nervousness behind what he hoped was a very sensible expression. It was difficult, though, to keep his face in this stiff and serious expression for the amount of time it was taking for the bell to be answered.

Gramps looked puzzled and tried again. Again a loud chime inside the house, but no sound of human activity. Clearly no one was going to open the door. Gramps stepped back down to the drive to look at the house better.

'Strange. No windows open, no cars, and absolutely no sign of life.' He turned and looked at Ben. 'It couldn't possibly have been a dream, could it?'

'No it couldn't!' Ben's voice was hot with indignation. 'Maybe you think Rory was having the same dream as me.' He stomped off down the drive towards the car.

Then it occurred to him that though there was nobody at the house there might be someone round at the barns or stables. Sure enough, he'd hardly turned into the lane they had taken the night before when a large tractor approached him. He looked up at the man driving it.

'Excuse me. Do you know where Mr Corbridge is? There's no answer at the house.'

'He's off at County Fair for a day or two.' Then the man squinted at Ben suspiciously. 'Who shall I say was looking for him?'

'Oh I . . . It's all right. I'll come back. Has all the family gone with him, then?'

'No. Shouldn't have thought so. No idea where they are. You off now, then?' He looked reassured to see Gramps approaching in the car.

'Yes. Thanks,' said Ben and went over to Gramps. He got into the car and slumped into the passenger seat.

'Mr Corbridge has gone to the County Fair, and the tractor driver doesn't know where the family is.'

'Mysterious, eh? What shall we do now? No point hanging around here.' Gramps glanced at Ben who was frowning miserably.

'Don't know, Gramps. Well, Rory and I were going to sort out the flyers today. Suppose I should make a start without her.' The heaviness and greyness he was feeling was in his voice too. Was he ever going to be able to make it up to her?

'Maybe go round to her or phone and tell her you've been up to Broadacres to apologise and that there's no one there. She might have heard something from Vanessa.'

'But if she hasn't she'll feel even worse, won't she? The two of them are always texting.'

'Well, let's just see. First, I think, I'll make us some hot chocolate. We'll feel better with something inside us.'

Ben doubted it.

As they approached Conkers, they saw a figure sitting on the doorstep writing a note. She looked up as soon as she heard the car.

'Good luck, Ben. I'll make that three hot chocolates.' He gave Rory a friendly wave and disappeared into the house.

Rory came straight over to Ben. 'Sorry I was stroppy and went off last night. It wasn't really your fault. Well, it sort of was, but you did try to protect me.'

'It's me that's sorry. I should never have let you come. It's a total mess. We've just been up to Broadacres so I could apologise but there's no one there. Well, someone on a tractor, but he said they'd all gone away.'

'What? Vanessa didn't say anything about going away. In fact, when I told her that we were doing the Big BuzZ she said she'd help us with the publicity. Course now she'll be thinking I was just using her to help us break in.'

'Seriously? She can't think that just because of one day! You were friends with her before you even knew me.'

'Well, she probably thinks it was very sneaky of me to go up there at night. And her parents must be livid, mustn't they? Well, Mr Corbridge certainly was. I've never seen him like that. Probably when he went back to the house Mrs Corbridge said that I wasn't a suitable friend for Vanessa and took her away somewhere till I go home. They've got a flat in London and she's got loads of cousins there.'

Gramps arrived with a tray in time to hear the end of her sentence and to see from their faces that, even if the two of them had made up, it hadn't raised their spirits.

'Look, you two, don't meet trouble halfway.'

'What on earth is that supposed to mean, Gramps?'

'Until you know for a fact that something bad has happened, don't start worrying about it. There's any number of explanations why they've gone away. She'll probably be in touch soon to tell you. Now try some of this. Bound to banish the blues.'

Rory looked puzzled.

'Gramps means it will cheer you up.' Ben sighed. He didn't look convinced. 'Well, try it, anyway. He does make wicked hot chocolate – with real dark chocolate, not powder.'

'Yes, Rory. You both need your energy today. You've an awful lot of work to do. People take months planning and preparing for fetes. We've just got a couple of weeks. Start by making a list I'd say.'

Chapter Twenty One

 Gramps and Ben had collected the flyers and posters and decided to take them straight round to Chris. Rory came out as soon as she heard the car.

'Hi, Rory. We're just back from the printers,' Ben announced. 'Your book looks wicked.'

'Good. I mean thanks.' Her voice was flat.

'So – no news?'

'If you mean has Vanessa called – no she hasn't.'

Busy as they had been in the last two days, Rory's mind had kept going back to the mystery of Vanessa's disappearance. Whatever explanation they'd managed to come up with to explain her vanishing so suddenly, they couldn't explain her silence.

'It's obvious she never wants to speak to me again,' was Rory's gloomy conclusion. And it seemed that even the idea of seeing her story in print couldn't cheer her up.

'Sorry.'

'Okay, Ben. I think you can stop saying that now. It's really not helping. Look, now you've got the flyers we'd better get going.'

'Right now?'

'Yeah. Chris suggested we head into town and then go around all the large carparks putting them on the windscreens. He's got some shopping to do so he'll give us a lift.'

Chris dropped them in the car park of the largest supermarket.

'I'll be about twenty minutes. Then we can go over to the other side of town where the retail park is.' He drove off.

'You start this end, Rory. I'll go to the other side.' Ben divided the flyers and gave her half.

As she took them, she caught sight of a tall blonde girl standing next to an even taller blonde woman. It seemed as if she'd been looking at them.

'Look, Ben, I'm sure that's Vanessa,' Rory cried out in surprise. But the girl had turned away and was speaking to the woman. 'It is her. She must have seen me and now she's ignoring me.' All the excitement had gone out of her voice.

'Don't think so,' said Ben, for Vanessa had now left her mother and was weaving her way at top speed through the rows of cars towards them. Rory shot off to meet her.

The two girls met in the middle with squeals of delight and excited questioning.

'What were you two getting up to in the shed?'

'Where have you been?' Ben could hear their excited voices even where he was standing.

'I'll explain in a minute. Why don't you start by telling me what you and Ben were up to the other night? You didn't half give us all a fright. I suppose this is Ben?'

He'd just joined them.

'Yes. Hi, Vanessa. We didn't mean to. We never realised an alarm would go off.'

'I bet you didn't.' Vanessa laughed. 'But that machinery of Dad's is jolly expensive. He thought some criminals were trying to steal it. A real fright he got. He came back in a stomping temper. Well, it was the second time in the night we'd been woken up. The first time it was a call to say Grandma had fallen and had to be taken into hospital.' Vanessa paused, very briefly, to take a breath.

'Mum wanted to go straight way, but Dad persuaded her that as Grandma was safely in hospital it was better to wait till the morning and go early. We'd only been back to sleep an hour when the alarm went off.' She paused and flicked her long, fair hair off her forehead – for the third time since she'd started speaking, Ben noticed.

'Anyway, never mind the alarm, what exactly *were* you doing poking around in our barn in the middle of the night?' Without waiting for an answer she was off again. 'Oh yes, don't tell me – investigating!'

Ben wondered who she reminded him of. Then he remembered. She was Frontoback in human form!

'As for why I didn't call – it was all a complete panic. Mum was in *such* a state. Half worried about Grandma, half cross about what happened. Mum's been saying for ages she shouldn't be living by herself. Wants her to come and live with us. There's plenty of room. She could have her own flat in our house.'

Ben was beginning to wonder how long this would go on and when they could get started on the leaflets, but Vanessa was clearly far from finished.

'So we got to the hospital and, before we went to find Grandma, we went to the loo. Mobile was in my back pocket. Yup. You've guessed it. Plopped into the toilet. I thought it would dry out okay. But no luck. It's a write off. Anyway, here we are – home for the moment. Well, Mum will be going back to London but I'm staying here. So I'm on for your BuzZy thing.'

Rory's freckly grin had made a comeback. She offered Vanessa some flyers. 'Okay, stop yapping. If you think your mum's going to be in the supermarket for a while, you could start with these. We've got to get them on all the cars in here.'

With the three of them going at top speed they managed to get around the carpark before there was any sign of Vanessa's mother.

'Let's go and meet Mum at the exit. She'll have bought some biscuits or something and I'm starving.'

Ben wasn't sure that this was at all a good idea. He certainly had room for a biscuit or two but he was in no hurry at all to meet Vanessa's mum.

'We arranged we'd meet Chris at the other carpark by the cinema and leisure centre. We should probably go and....'

'But we've got ten minutes,' Rory interrupted. Ben frowned at her and hoped she'd get the message. Vanessa certainly did.

'Look, Ben, don't worry about Mum. Luckily, when Rory and I went riding, she told me what you've been doing. So when Mum started off in the car about what on earth the two of you were doing breaking in, she'd always thought Rory was such a nice girl and all that, I explained what you've both been up to. Well, you know, about Ben being on a mission to solve the mystery of bee disappearances and your project. I think she was impressed actually. She knows more than you'd think about the dangers of using insecticides and stuff. Well, we all get to hear about it, you see, when Dad and Andy have one of their massive arguments.'

'Andy?' asked Ben.

'My brother Andrew. He's studying land management at university. He's right with you about chemicals. He thinks they're terrible for the soil too. You should come and have a word with him some time. He's away with friends, but he'll be back soon.' She didn't wait for a response. 'Want to hear how he and Dad go at each other?' She opened her eyes wide so that their whites showed, her chin jutted forward and a stream of angry words burst forth: 'All very fine, you coming back home with all your fancy ideas about organic farming, but who is the one *paying* for you to go to university, *paying* for your car, *paying* for Vanessa's horses? Where exactly do you think the money will be coming from if we stop using pesticides?'

Vanessa's imitation of Mr Corbridge was very funny. She then continued in her own voice, just a little deeper and slower: 'You're just a chemicals addict, Dad. Yuh. Those chemicals companies have got you so, like, addicted. You probably even believe their stuff about how you can get better crops with their products. How they're feeding the world's growing population. Yuh right. When their stuff is actually *ruining* the soil.'

Ben and Rory were grinning at Vanessa's mimicry.

'But where is your dad?' asked Ben. 'I came up to your house to apologise and someone told me he was away.'

'Well, he's back now. And sounds like a good idea coming to explain. You need him on your side if you want to help your grandpa's bees. He may get very fierce when he gets angry, but he won't eat you.' She spotted her mother coming out of the supermarket with a loaded trolley. 'Bring him a jar of honey when you come.' She was laughing. 'Okay, see you soon, then.'

Chapter Twenty Two

Ben and Mr Corbridge were looking at each other across Mr Corbridge's desk. A pot of Gramps's honey stood on the desk between them. If Vanessa had thought it might sweeten Mr Corbridge's temper, she'd been wrong.

Now that Mr Corbridge's eyes were not bulging, his face was not unpleasant. His voice, though, was not at all friendly.

'All very fine bringing me honey, Ben, but the fact remains that this is a very serious matter. You're extremely lucky I didn't call the police. If Rory hadn't been with you, I probably would have. I don't think they take very kindly to youngsters trespassing — worse, breaking in. You'd have had a police record.'

That possibility had never entered Ben's head. His guts went watery and, when he tried to speak, he found his tongue had become a useless lump in his mouth.

'I'm-I'm—' he stammered, but Mr Corbridge didn't wait to see if he could manage to finish his sentence.

'Fancy yourself a private investigator, my daughter tells me. And you suspected me of breaking the law, did you? Using neonicotinoids when there's a ban on? Never stopped to think, did you, that if you found them in the barn they could have been there since before they were banned? With all your poking around, it never occurred to you that perhaps they were stuck hidden away right at the back of the barn precisely because I haven't been using them.'

Ben tried again to speak. 'I really am very sorry, Mr Corbridge. Very, very sorry,' he managed feebly, for he felt that by now he'd worn any meaning out of the word.

'You see the thing is, Mr Corbridge . . .' But what was the thing? The words Ben had prepared disappeared from his head.

Then he had a stroke of inspiration. 'The thing is,' he started again more confidently, 'it's no help that you've stopped using imidacloprid. The harm's already been done. It stays in the soil. It gets into the water system and then –' he paused – 'the wildflowers next to your field are contaminated by them. And that's what's poisoned Gramps's bees.'

Whew. He'd got the words out and managed to silence Mr Corbridge. He still looked severe, but he seemed to be thinking about what Ben had said. His tone was no longer threatening when he spoke again.

'Ben, there's no actual proof that neonicotinoids kill bees. There are plenty of other things that affect the bees' health.'

Indignation bubbled up in Ben when he heard Mr Corbridge's words. He thought of the sick and hungry bees in the hive. He thought of the foragers coming back ill and falling down dead. He thought of Gramps's half-empty hives and he burst out angrily, 'That's just not true, Mr Corbridge. Yes, of course there are lots of things that are harmful to bees as well as neonicotinoids. It's really a hard life being a bee, I can tell you. And if they're already weak because of the diseases they get, and short of food because of all the massive fields now with only one crop, well, they're much too weak to be able to cope with poisons too.' Words were now pouring out of Ben in a torrent of anger. 'And that's what imidacloprid is – a poison.'

His voice had risen. He had completely forgotten about being frightened of Mr Corbridge.

'The only scientists who defend the use of pesticides are the ones who work for the chemical companies that produce them. They're not called industry friendly for nothing. But all the other scientists agree that bees are being poisoned by these products. Look, I've brought something to show you.' He scuffled in his rucksack and produced the article by the Professor at Sussex University that he'd found and thrust it on to the desk.

'Have a look at that. You might have stopped using neonics, Mr Corbridge, but maybe it's too late. Well, too late for Gramps's bees anyway. Most of them are dead already.'

Mr Corbridge was frowning but made no attempt to interrupt Ben who clearly was not finished.

'When you've had a look, you'll see for yourself. The imadocloprid stays in the hedgerows and is in the pollen of wildflowers the bees are foraging in.' Ben's indignation had sent a hot, red flush into his cheeks. 'Worse, it gets mixed up with other things you spray, weedkiller and stuff, and that makes a chemical cocktail. Do you know what that means, Mr Corbridge?' He paused a moment. 'It means the pesticides become a thousand times more dangerous. Look, it's all in that article. If you read it, maybe you'll believe me.'

Chapter Twenty Three

Gramps was weeding when Ben got back. He looked up as he heard Ben's bike crunching on the gravel. 'You were a while, Ben. How did it go?'

'Well, he ranted on at me for a while. Told me he could have called the police. Then he claimed there was no proof the neonics had been killing the bees anyway. So I lost it and started to have a massive go at him.'

'Great. That was your idea of apologising and making the peace was it?'

'Will you let me finish, Gramps? He did actually listen in the end. I showed him the article I found and Rory's book and, guess what, he said leave them with him and he'd have a look.'

Gramps nodded slowly and smiled. 'Well, well. That's a surprise.'

'Wait – this'll really surprise you – in the end he got quite pleasant and said he'd heard about our Big BuzZ next week and thought we might like to know that they were having an

Open Farm afternoon this weekend.'

'And so?'

'Well, seems like they have loads of visitors because people who are on holiday around here like to see the cows being milked and all that. And then, of course, they have a homemade tea. I bet that's the real draw. Anyway, they're usually packed out, he said.'

'Still don't see how that helps us.'

'Well, he suggested I come up at the weekend and put flyers on all the cars in their car park. That was pretty decent, hey? And if families think it's fun to go looking around farms, well, they're bound to be excited when they read about all the games we're going to have and the bouncy castle and everything.'

'Well, that is a result, Ben. So why the serious face?'

'Dunno. I suppose I was just thinking that it's all very well that he's trying to be helpful and so now we'll get a load more people to the Big BuzZ, but how's that going help us get the bees back? And what's the point of you replacing them, Gramps, when they're just going to go off foraging over at Broadacres – happily sucking up a load of toxic cocktails?'

Ben felt tears pricking behind his eyes. He blinked them back.

'And even if he thinks about it all and decides not to use imadacloprid again, well, Gramps, how does that help us? It's obvious your hives aren't safe here at the moment. It's just pointless giving them sugar fondant. They're all going to die anyway.' He slumped down full length on to the ground, burying his face in the grass to hide his tears of frustration. He felt like an old balloon whose air had seeped away.

Gramps sat down beside him. 'Well, if that's the problem I've some good news for you. In fact, Ben, I should to start by thanking you – because none of this would have happened if it wasn't for you.'

'None of what?' came Ben's muffled voice from out of the grass.

'None of what I'm just about to tell you. It's really thanks to you I made it up with Chris. You were dead right: he's a great bloke. And then there's Seb Stringfellow. Only knew him to say hello to before.'

Ben emerged from the grass, smiling as he thought of how they'd got to know Stringfellow.

'Is that the news you said you had?'

'No. There's something else. You know how decent Chris has been about lending me a hive and giving me a swarm?' continued Gramps.

'Yup.'

'It made me think. We all

agreed, you remember, that his bees are safer where he lives because he's well away from any pesticide-spraying landowner. So, I thought that maybe Seb would be happy to keep my hives on his smallholding for the time being. With all the different crops he has during the year, my bees are going to think they're in bee paradise!'

'And you've already asked him?'

'Yup. It's a done deal. Works well for him too, because they'll be busy pollinating all his produce. So, Ben, it's all down to you really.'

Ben felt the black cloud lift off his spirits. Apparently things weren't so desperate after all. But Gramps hadn't finished.

'So I just wanted to say I'm proud of you. Seems like you've really taken on board what I said about the importance of activism.'

'You mean all it takes for evil to triumph is for the good to do nothing?' Ben grinned at Gramps.

'What a memory you've got, Ben. Couldn't be teasing your preachy old grandpa, by any chance?'

'I'm really not teasing, Gramps. I didn't get it when you said if you're not part of the solution you're part of the problem. I do now, though. I can see there's just no point grumbling about useless governments and evil multinationals. If we don't take action against them, well, we're sort of supporting them.'

Gramps was shaking his head, but his expression was admiring. He gave Ben's shoulder a squeeze. As he spoke there seemed to be something obstructing his throat.

'You know, Ben, it's because of you I care so

much. I want you to be able to enjoy the things that have made my life happy and which are disappearing so fast.'

What on earth is Gramps on about? thought Ben, looking at him blankly. Loads of the things he enjoyed hadn't even been invented when Gramps was young.

'What do you mean, Gramps? What's disappearing so fast?'

'I mean I'd like for there still to be butterflies and frogs around for you to see, and the sound of birds singing and crickets chirping. The way wildlife is vanishing, you'll soon have to go and see them in zoos.'

Gramps put his arm round Ben's shoulders. 'Now, about Mr Corbridge.'

Ben's heart sank. Flipping heck. 'I thought we'd finished with him,' he muttered under his breath.

'Know what?' Gramps continued. 'I don't think it matters that you lost it with him. I think the fact you care so much and have found out so much really impressed him.'

'Maybe. But what about my plan to be a private investigator, Gramps? I haven't found anything that someone somewhere didn't know about already!'

'Not sure that's important Ben. It's your persistence at finding out the truth that matters. And important truths, too, that some people would like to hide. So tell me, instead of becoming a special investigator, what do you think about becoming an investigative journalist?'

Chapter Twenty Four

 As they'd hoped, it had turned out to be a gloriously sunny day and people were pouring into Gramps's huge field and queuing to pay for entrance.

Many of the children enjoying the different stalls already had bee faces and Rory and Ben had handed over the face-painting stall to Vanessa and a friend of hers so that they could have a break.

Now that Rory didn't have to keep a smile on her face for the customers it was clear to Ben that she wasn't very happy.

'Quit worrying, Rory. Just because the reporters haven't arrived doesn't mean they're not coming. They've probably got other events they have to cover too.'

'Well, if they don't turn up soon they might as well not bother.'

'Oh, come on, don't exaggerate. There's still plenty of time. There's something else bothering you, isn't there?'

'Well, I know it's not her fault and all that, but it's really disappointing about Mum not coming today like she promised.'

'But you said she had a great opportunity to understudy for one of the dancers in Giselle and she'll be performing in the National Opera House.'

'I know, I know. I should be pleased for her. I am really. But you know . . .' She closed her eyes and sniffed as if she was holding back tears.

'Come on, let's take some photos and send them to her. She's going to be so proud of you, Rory. Or what about a video of Stringfellow? In fact, we could have a go at *Knock Off a Big Boy* ourselves now. We've worked hard enough.'

'Okay, you're on.'

They joined the queue and watched the game while waiting.

A boy in the circle had just grabbed the sack and he swung it hard towards Stringfellow. But Stringfellow caught it easily and pushed it back to topple a small boy from his log.

'That's him out,' said Rory.

As the sack swung back to the centre, Stringfellow managed to catch it again and he hurled it at a girl this time. She struggled to get hold of it, but lost her footing and fell off too.

'Wow. Who'd have thought Stringfellow would be so good at this,' said Rory. 'Now what's going to happen is the children will get really fed up and put their friends off trying.'

'You're being such a worry bug this afternoon. There've been queues for this all afternoon. And you know why? This lot have just started the game, but the players soon realise they have to use tactics if they're going to beat Stringfellow.'

'Oh yeah, right, *tactics*. It's a flipping sack of hay, Ben, not a war game!'

'Just watch.'

'I am,' said Rory gloomily as a skinny girl with a ponytail was the next to overbalance and land on the ground.

'Just wait a minute,' said Ben. He'd noticed that the remaining players were exchanging meaningful glances across the ring. The next player to get the sack didn't attempt to hit Stringfellow, but

threw the sack past him and into the arms of a skinny boy on the other side of the circle.

'Wasted throw,' snorted Rory, but the skinny boy who'd caught it threw it hard at Stringfellow's back.

Stringfellow, surprised as the sack whammed into him from behind him, lost his footing and nearly tumbled off his platform. As it sailed on, a quick-witted girl got hold of it and lobbed it over to a girl opposite her. She caught it quickly and before Stringfellow had a chance to turn round and attempt to catch it she had thrown it into his back again. Again he teetered – this time on the very edge of the platform and only just regained his balance. The children started cheering.

'See what I mean? Once they gang up like that and keep attacking him from behind, his size and big platform aren't such an advantage, are they?'

But then he noticed that Rory was no longer paying any attention to the game.

'Look at those two over there, the ones with cameras – one's tall, the other's sort of round. I bet that's them. I've got to keep an eye on them.'

While Ben watched the end of the game, Rory watched Little and Large as they moved from cake stall to ice cream stall, sampling everything as they went.

'Ben, I can't wait here any longer. If it is them, I've got to make sure that they take photos of Barty and Stringfellow.' And she was gone.

Moments later, she'd caught up with them drinking beer at the refreshments.

'Excuse me. Are you the press?' She smiled at them sweetly, masking her disapproval that they seemed to be treating the Big BuzZ as a large tea party.

'Would you, by any chance, be Aurora?' the taller man asked.

'That's right.'

'And you've organised this Big BuzZ with your grandfather.'

'Well, it's Ben's grandfather, actually, and this is his field. My uncle and I are helping, though.'

'Well, a splendid effort I must say. We've enjoyed it very much.'

'Enjoyed it?'

'Yes. Pity we've got to go, but we've another local event to cover.'

'But you want some photos of the games, don't you? So you can explain to your readers how the Big BuzZ is all about helping people to understand about how dangerous pesticides are to bees . . .'

'Well now, my dear, I think we've actually got all we need already. And we've got to think of our readers, remember. Lots of farmers and landowners you see.' He turned to his companion.

'What do you think, Jeff? This ban-the-neonicotinoids business isn't going to play very well with them, is it? I really think we should be off now.'

He turned back to Rory as Ben ran up to join them. 'Look, I just need to visit the boys' room. How about we have a nice photo of you and – Bill was it you said? – when I get back.'

Rory face was flushed as she watched him go and her green eyes were sparking with anger. 'He just might as well not have bothered to come.'

Till now Rory had been addressing her comments to Frank. Tall and full of his own importance, she imagined he was the chief reporter and the one she needed to convince. But as he strode off she turned to Jeff, a quiet and round-faced man – his assistant she supposed – and asked, rather crossly, 'So what's he talking about anyway – not playing well with farmers and landowners? What's that supposed to mean?'

Jeff explained, 'What Frank means, I think, is that unfortunately some of our readers will be the very people who are using neonicotinoids. And they won't be too happy to see them criticised.'

'Then they're exactly the people who *need* to know. Oh please, Jeff, you've got to help us persuade Frank.'

'Doubt I'll be able to do that I'm afraid. "Have to keep our readers happy you know." That's what the proprietors, they're the newspapers owners, you know, keep saying. Could be out of our jobs if we don't. All this Big Boy stuff – they won't like it. Newspaper owners are rather big boys themselves . . .'

He stopped for a moment, taking in Ben and Rory's downcast faces.

'Look, you two, I'm just explaining why it's unlikely I could persuade Frank. The magazines he works for – *Field and Furrow, Hare and Hounds* – well, you can guess who would be reading them: the big landowners. But I'm with the local paper, *The Barsetshire Bugle*. It has a more general readership so perhaps I'll hang about a bit and you can fill me in on what's been going on. How about that?'

Rory now seemed ready to throw her arms around him and give him a hug. Ben just looked at him hopefully. 'Even better, you could come with us and see the empty hives for yourself and I'll explain everything.'

Chapter Twenty Five

 Ben and Gramps were loading dustbin bags with litter. They'd filled three already and had only been working in a small patch of the field.

'I'm shattered. I need a break,' said Ben, and flung himself down on the grass. 'Phew. It doesn't seem to agree with me being woken up like that, Gramps, on a Sunday morning.'

'Morning, Ben? Eleven thirty? Practically the afternoon.'

'Whatever,' said Ben, not stirring from his position.

A voice hailed them from the other side of the field. 'Hi there. Here comes the clear-up team.' Chris was getting out of his car.

'Team?' Gramps grinned. There was no sign of anyone else.

Chris looked behind him into the car. 'Don't say she's gone back to sleep again. Had the devil of a job getting her out of bed to get here at all.'

'Well, this one isn't exactly a cleaning tornado.' Gramps motioned to Ben, still supine on the grass.

Rory got out of the car, blearily, and stumbled towards them.

'I need coffee,' she said, slumping down beside Ben.

Chris raised his eyebrows and muttered to Toby. 'Allowed it at home on Sundays, she claims.'

'Hey, you two,' said Gramps. 'What happened to our deal? "We'll leave the field so nobody could guess that anything had happened in it?" Remember?'

'Yes, but it can wait a bit, can't it, Gramps?' Ben was dragging himself reluctantly into a sitting position. As he did so, he saw figures crossing the field toward them. They must have come by way of the house. He smiled in recognition. It looked like the kids they'd got friendly with towards the end of the Big BuzZ yesterday. They'd signed up for the coach to go to London for the demonstration. Yes, Laura, who Rory had known already, Eddie, Tom . . . but who were those older-looking ones heading towards them? One of them looked somehow familiar.

Then he twigged. Of course! The tall, lanky one with fair hair must be Vanessa's brother. He was already greeting Gramps.

'Hello, Mr Busby. Great do you put on yesterday! Beat our open day, I reckon. I was really sorry that I couldn't make it earlier.'

Make it earlier? Ben hadn't seen him at all. Maybe he'd arrived when he and Rory were showing Gramps's beehives to Jeff?

Andy had turned to him now. 'So you must be Ben. I've been looking forward to meeting you.' He was grinning at him. 'Really took on my dad, I hear.'

Ben felt his face getting warm. He hadn't seen Mr Corbridge since their heated conversation.

'Was he livid?'

'No – just loved being called a mass murderer of insects.'

He saw Ben's horrified face. 'Only kidding. No, in fact, he could see where you were coming from. Showed me the stuff you left too. So fact is I'm grateful to you, Ben. I think you've helped me in my struggle.'

'What struggle?'

'I'm trying to get Dad to change Broadacres into a farm that will still be sustainable when he retires and I take over. I probably don't need to tell you that the pesticides and fertilisers harming your bees aren't doing much for the soil up there either. Once upon a time, farmers rotated the crops so that they always had some fields growing clover to nourish the soil – and the bees! Well, I'm not trying to get Dad back to that exactly. But I have persuaded him to introduce herbal leys . . .'

Ben's eyebrow shot up. What on earth was Andy talking about?

'Sorry, Ben. I'm getting a bit technical. Comes of mixing with all these would-be farmers.' He glanced at his friends who were now busy filling dustbin bags. 'It means having meadows growing wild flowers and then letting the cows graze on them. Much nicer for the cows than being indoors, and great for the soil. Lovely mix of cow poo and wild flowers gets trampled in by the cows. And great for insects too obviously.'

'Vanessa told us that your dad said he couldn't afford to change to organic farming.'

'Well, this way he can do it gradually, can't he? But it's certainly the way forward for Broadacres. When he goes on about how he wouldn't be able to keep us in the luxury to which we're accustomed, I tell him he's actually killing the goose that lays the golden egg.' He looked at Ben's blank face. 'I mean he should take care of the soil instead of worrying about profits all the time. Goose equals soil, get it?'

Ben nodded. 'That sounds like what happened in Rory's story.'

'Dead right. Yes, what Rory wrote really made him think, and –' He stopped abruptly and then exclaimed, 'My goodness, who's that who's just turned up? Look, she's over there greeting Chris.' Ben turned to see a glamorous woman standing in front of her little car. Her red hair was swept up into a loose coil, and she was wearing a shimmery green dress, and large sunglasses.

'Doesn't exactly look as if she's come to join the clear-up team, does she?' Andy grinned.

Rory had jumped and was running towards her. Andy and Ben followed slowly.

'So her mum's turned up. Rory was pretty upset yesterday when she didn't get to the BuzZ. Had to stay in London to perform in *Giselle*. She was understudying one of the Wilis and . . .'

An enormous grin had spread over Andy's face. 'Some sort of modern ballet, is it? Dancing willies, I mean? Could she get us tickets, do you think?'

Ben burst out laughing. 'Wilis, Andy. You know, they lure men to their death.'

Andy was clearly even more amused by this explanation. 'Well, I'd certainly like to see that!'

'I don't think so.' Ben was laughing so much his insides were hurting. 'It's a bunch of spirits in long, floaty ballet skirts who surround young men and sort of dance them to death. They're the Wilis, you see. W I L I S,' he spelt out.

'Ah,' said Andy, still smiling. They had now reached the little group around Rory's mum and she immediately greeted Ben.

'You must be Ben – champion of the bees and investigator extraordinaire!'

Ben felt himself going red. What on earth had Rory been telling her mother?

'Er, pleased to meet you.' Rory's mum was already turning her gaze to the little group that had gathered around her.

'Wonderful effort from you all. And some of you are coming up to London, too, I gather, for the Support the Bees demonstration. Well, my lovelies, I reckon I could get some of the ballet company to come along as well. Musicians too, maybe. We've got a hive on top of the opera house, you know. Frightfully fashionable, bees, at the moment!' She turned and tilted her head towards Gramps, widening her eyes appealingly.

'Toby, you couldn't be an absolute darling and raise me a cup of coffee, could you? I had a rather late night last night and a very early start this morning.'

'I certainly could find you one and even a slice of cake to go with it. Come this way Carina. You too, Rory,' he said, leading the way towards the house.

Andy turned to Vanessa. 'Could be fun to see Rory's mum dancing sometime.'

'Well, I don't think *Giselle* is the one for you. She's going to be in *Romeo and Juliet* this autumn. Lots of sword fights and drama. Much more up your street. What?' she asked, looking at their faces. They were still grinning in secret amusement.

Chris came over to where they were talking. 'Seb's coming up with his van in a minute to take the trestles back to the

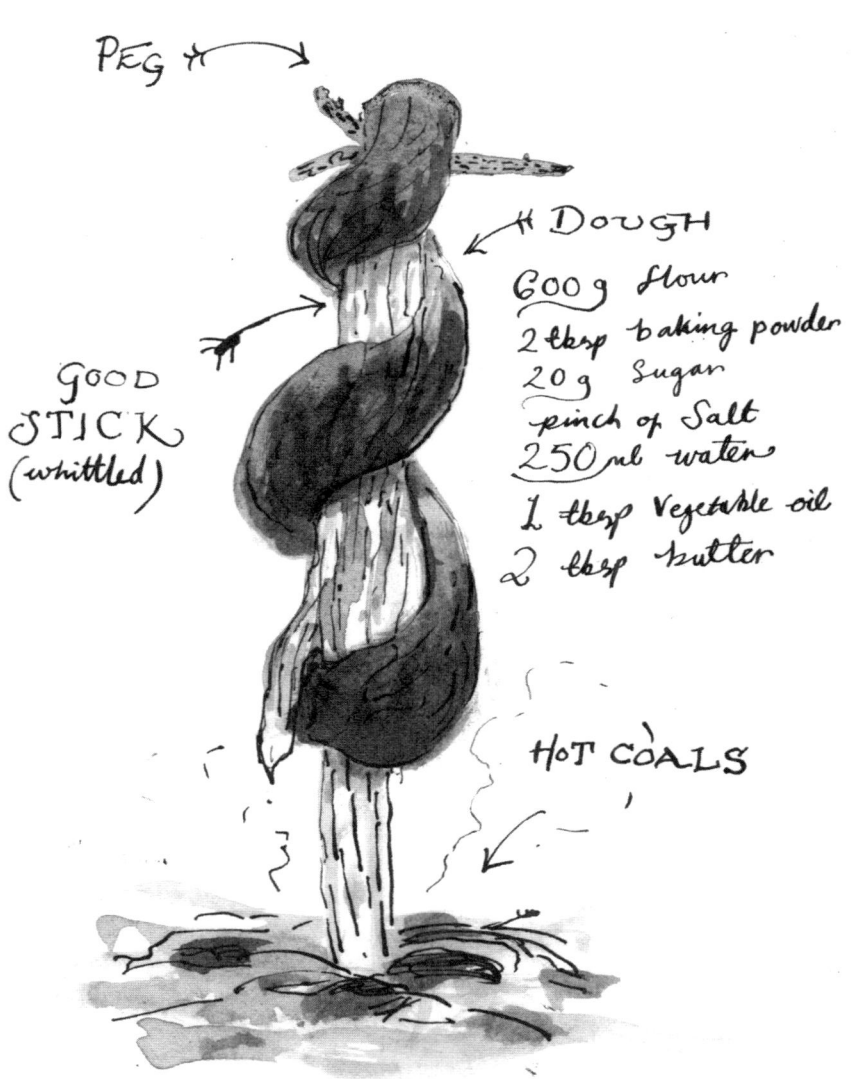

village hall. With all this help we'll have the clear-up done in no time. How about when we get back we make a bonfire and bake some stick bread for everyone? You could get some drinks out in the meantime, Ben. Plenty left from yesterday.'

It was early evening. Rory and Chris had gone home and made pasta for Carina's dinner and waved her off back to London. They decided to have a short cycle ride. The sun was low in the sky, casting flickering shadows on the lane where there were groups of trees, and pools of dappled golden light where there were none.

'He will, he won't, he will, he won't,' Rory was intoning as light alternated with shade.

'Am I allowed to ask who will or won't?'

'I was counting, Chris. Shadows he won't. Light and he will. Now you've made me lose count.'

'Sorry. Want to carry on or explain to me?'

'Jeff – that reporter I told you about. Will he write anything useful for his paper or not?'

'Perhaps not the most scientific way of establishing probability.'

'And even if he does he might write the kind of soppy thing like there usually is for village fêtes. You know – *Buzzy event at Lower Melbury. Wonderful weather brought out a big crowd . . . lots of stalls with local produce . . . plenty of entertainment for the kids* – that kind of stuff.'

'Doesn't sound bad. He might mention my honey cake too. Someone did take a picture.'

'You're teasing, aren't you? Not bad! It would be . . .' She searched for an adjective strong enough that wouldn't offend Chris. 'It would be just flipping useless.'

'Well, I'm sorry you feel like that because I must admit you've got the tone of our local paper to a T. The biggest excitement is usually who has grown the largest turnip. But you haven't got long to wait. Local paper comes out Thursday.'

Not for the first time, Rory thought that adults had a completely different sense of time. It was Monday night and Thursday seemed an eternity away.

Chapter Twenty Six

A clunking sound woke Ben. He lay still a moment. There it was again. The sound of something hitting glass. Someone had thrown something against the window. Then he heard his name being called. He got out of bed, went to the window and pulled the curtain aside to see Rory below, waving. He opened the window.

'Came round the back so's not to wake your grandpa.'

'What have you got there?'

'The paper of course.'

'But the shop can't be open yet.'

'Well, no – but the papers had arrived and they were there sorting them out.'

'So?'

She shrugged. 'At least he has written *something* and there are some photos. Chris will be pleased anyway.'

'I'm coming down.'

Ben let Rory in, but when she handed the paper over her usually animated face was expressionless.

'Don't bother looking on the front page,' was all she said.

Ben opened the paper on the kitchen table and started leafing through. Nothing, nothing, nothing. It was when he reached the centre pages that he caught sight of a photo of Barty – his massive water gun quite useless as he tried to avoid a hail of wet sponges. His eyes next went to the headline and his eyes grew large.

'You were having me on, weren't you? This is epic.'

'Didn't want to spoil the surprise, but it's not bad, is it?' Rory's grin was enormous. 'Come on, let me have a look too. I only had a quick peep before because I wanted to read it with you.'

12-year-old Ben makes shocking discovery

Ben's annual visit to his grandfather, local beekeeper Toby Busby, has this year been marred by a very nasty shock. More than 80% of his grandfather's bees have disappeared – and even those that remain are struggling to survive.

Ben says that he wanted to help his grandfather make sure that the remaining bees didn't die too. He started to learn about the reasons for bee losses and the connection with neonicotinoids. 'This is a new kind of pesticide that doesn't kill bees outright, so it's very hard to prove how dangerous they are. But, though the effects of neonicotinoids are slow, in the end they are absolutely deadly,' he declares.

Ben and his friend Rory decided to hold Big BuzZ – a fun day out that informed people about the threats to bees and helped them understand how vital they are to humans. As plans progressed, however, their ambitions grew.

Ben and the Power of Purchase

'People need to understand,' says Ben, 'that they can do much more than plant bee-friendly seeds if they want to help the bees. They can help by not using these fertilisers and pesticides that are not only killing bees – but birds and animals too.'

Though initially concerned about bees, Ben found himself worried about the danger to humans as these products find their way into the water system. It is children's health especially that will suffer, he has discovered.

'There are so many health-and-safety rules nowadays that people believe that the government protects us from all danger. Not so', says Ben. 'When it comes to some very serious threats, they're very slow to act.'

A Very BuZzy Garden Fête

Included among the stalls you expect to find at a garden fête, Ben and Rory came up with some rather original activities to emphasise the danger of big business. Competing against each other in the tug of war were two unusual teams, *Profit Rules OK?* versus *People Power*, whilst in *Sock it to the Multinationals* the youngsters, by combining forces, had the opportunity to topple the Big Boys in an amusing version of a medieval game.

Kid Power – the Way to Go

'Making sure your parents only buy products for the garden that *don't* harm wildlife or have harmful effects on human health is just one way children can help,' Rory suggests. 'We should share ideas on social media. If adults aren't doing enough to protect us, we just have to act for ourselves and demand better laws to protect the planet.'

'Yes,' agreed Ben. 'There's already a group of British children campaigning against climate change, and in India there's a girl our age who's prosecuting the Indian government for permitting the terrible levels of pollution there.

Ecocide, you know. It's the new crime and I bet it will be youngsters who bring the perpetrators to justice!'

When they'd finished reading, they sat a moment sharing wide grins.

'Satisfied, Rory?'

'Couldn't have hoped for better – well, from a local paper anyway.'

'Rory!'

'No, I mean it. We'll make the national press next time! Just wait till we get to London.'

'How about we go and show this to Gramps? He should be up by now.'

'In a sec, but while we're by ourselves there's something I need to ask you. It's about how you metamorphosed . . .'

Ah yes, thought Ben. *Now for the grilling.*

'What about it, then? You think it was a dream too, don't you?'

'Of course I don't think it was a dream!' Rory exclaimed. 'Dreams keep shifting from one thing to another. And just when something particularly strange or exciting happens you wake up. And then you want to tell someone about it and it all kind of melts. Like when you try to look at a snowflake and it just dissolves in your hand.'

Rory shook her head. 'But you remember everything that happened and all the details – so it couldn't possibly have been a dream. Anyway, what I was trying to ask you about transforming was – well, next time we'll do it together, agreed?'

'Agreed. But there's one little problem, Rory. Remember I told you that Gramps has hidden all the royal jelly?'

Rory looked at him, her eyes sparkling. 'Well, what a laugh if he thinks that's going to stop us!'

Turn over to Ben's Bee Book

Ben's Bee Book

by BEN
ROOOPS.

Role of the Queen Bee

The queen is the largest bee in the colony and lays all the eggs in the hive.

It is the worker bees who decide which egg will become a queen. That egg is put in a larger cell and the larva which emerges is fed on royal jelly.

Soon after the queen emerges from her cell as an adult she makes several mating flights. This means that she flies out of the hive followed by 13-18 drone bees. During the flight, she will mate with the drones and receive millions of sperm cells to fertilize the eggs she will later lay. These sperm cells last all her life — two to five years on average.

She spends her entire life just laying eggs — up to 3,000 in one day. This means she lays the equivalent of her body weight every couple of hours.

Royal Jelly

Royal jelly is the substance which worker bees produce from glands in their heads to feed the developing larvae. Worker bees are only given it for the first few days of their life, but those larvae which will become queens are fed only on royal jelly, and are given it often and in large quantities.

Just as a mother's milk protects her baby from all sorts of illnesses, royal jelly protects the developing larvae from infection. Because of this, and because queens grow to be much bigger than drones, many people believe it has benefits for humans too and, though it is expensive, they are prepared to pay for it.

Guarding the Hive

Guard bees constantly patrol the 'take-off' shelf outside the narrow entrance to the hive. No bee can enter without a security check. The guard will feel her antennae to be sure that she bears the hive's own particular odour.

If, however, a bee is suspected of being an intruder intending to steal honey, the guard releases alarm pheromones. The smell will immediately attract other guard bees that will attack and kill it.

ATTENTION

Worker bees' schedule

Young Workers: 1-12 days old

Clean cells

Nurse the larvae

Middle aged workers: 12-20 days old

Build the comb

Process and **Store** the nectar

Control hive temperature by flapping wings

Guard hive entrance

Remove dead bees

Mature workers: 20 days and more

Leave hive to fly off and forage

Collect nectar and pollen

Return to hive and process nectar

CAUTION

Under no circumstances may a worker bee younger than 20 days leave the hive

Role of the Worker Bee

85-90% of bees in a colony are worker bees. They are female but cannot lay eggs.

However, these industrious bees do almost all of the work in the hive. Although what they are known for is supplying the hive with nectar and pollen, they do not, in fact, leave the hive to go collecting, or foraging as it is called, until they are mature.

First, as young workers, and according to their age, they will have been responsible for a variety of tasks inside the hive. These are shown on the Worker Bees' Schedule.

They fly at a speed of 15 miles per hour and can travel about 5 miles from the hive on a single flight. If humans could fly this would be the equivalent of a human 'flying' from London to Geneva, or Edinburgh to Calais in one flight.

Pollen Sac

As well as sucking up nectar from flowers, the bees collect the pollen they have gathered on their furry bodies.

They comb it off their bodies into special baskets or pollen sacs on their hind legs and take it back to the hive.

Pollen Bread

When forager bees return to the hive the pollen contained in their pollen sacs is removed by other workers.

They moisten it with regurgitated honey and saliva which helps to preserve it and turns it into 'pollen bread'. It is then packed into cells near the nursery.

This protein rich food is then fed to larvae and is also eaten by young worker bees in the first ten days of their lives, to aid their development of their internal organs.

Waggle Dance

The scientist Karl von Frisch was the first person to discover that bees dance to inform other foragers where to find food.

In the more simple **round dance**, the dancer turns round to trace a circle and repeats the same circle, once to the right and once to the left several times. The purpose of this dance is to direct fellow foragers to a particularly rich source of nectar near to the hive — usually at a distance of between 50 and 100 metres.

The bees have another dance to encourage bees to visit a nectar source located further away from the hive. This is known as the **waggle dance**.

The dancing bee moves forward on the honeycomb in a straight line, then traces a half circle to return to the starting point. She repeats the straight line, this time following it by half circle to the left, thus forming a figure eight. She continues this pattern again and again.

Whilst running the short distance in a straight line, the dancing bee is waggling her abdomen very vigorously. This is the movement that gives the dance its name. As there may be many different kinds of flowers blooming at the same time, the bees who have discovered the richest source of food will dance the most energetically and so send out the largest number of foragers to this particular flower. In this way the pollination of these flowers is guaranteed and the beehive receives the best and sweetest nectar. Once the nectar at this source becomes scarce the dances stop and so no more workers are sent out to this species of flower.

The Asian Hornet

This large, bee-eating variety of hornet recently arrived in France from China and its numbers are increasing very rapidly.

Its rapacious appetite means that it is a very great threat to bees. It only takes one or two of them to destroy a hive of 30,000 bees in just over an hour.

In some parts of France 30% of hives have been lost to this ferocious insect which feeds it own young with bee larvae.

There is great concern that the rapidly increasing hornet population will spread to other European countries, including the UK.

Glyphosates

Glyphosates are present in the herbicides most widely used worldwide. They are used in agriculture by local councils and by the general public.

Because they enter the water system and poison the soil, they pose a risk to human health as well.

Because they are often sprayed on crops to dry them before harvesting they enter the human food chain. Traces have been found in flour, in bread etc.

Their use has already been discouraged or partially banned in several European countries.

Natural Beekeeping

The emphasis in natural beekeeping is on keeping healthy bees rather than on producing the maximum amount of honey.

It aims, therefore, to interfere in the lives of bees as little as possible. Traditional hives are supplied with pre-fabricated, rectangular frames — so the bees are obliged to build rectangular combs with a fixed cell size.

Natural beekeepers use hives with top-bars but no frames thus permitting the bees to construct the same shape of comb as they would in the wild. In the wild bees build heart-shaped combs. No product is put into the hive which could possibly be harmful to them, to humans or to the environment.

Honey is removed only when the bees have a surplus and never before the winter when the bees are likely to need it for themselves.

Lobbying

Lobbying is an attempt to influence government to support laws that give your organisation or industry an advantage. Individuals, non profit organisations and large multinational companies may all seek to promote their views in this way. Those who have most money generally have the most success.

'If we and the rest of the back-boned animals were to disappear overnight, the rest of the world would get on pretty well. But if the invertebrates were to disappear, the world's ecosystems would collapse.'

Sir David Attenborough

STOP PRESS!

MAJOR BLOW FOR MONSANTO

Last month a jury in San Francisco USA ruled that Monsanto was liable for a terminally ill man's cancer and awarded him $289 million in damages.

Lee Johnson, 46, is a father of three. He worked as a grounds keeper and pest manager for a school district just north of San Francisco. His position involved him spraying the herbicide Roundup to control weeds on school grounds.

When he took the stand he argued that his exposure to the chemicals caused non-Hodgkin lymphoma, a blood cell cancer. He told the jury of his pain and suffering as skin lesions took over his body. He stated that he would never have sprayed Roundup so near to school children had he known of the risks to children's health.

His lawyer stated that "Monsanto has known for decades that … Roundup could cause cancer."

The jury not only found that Monsanto's Roundup weedkiller caused his cancer but that Monsanto had "acted with malice or oppression".

Johnson, who has probably only months to live, is the first person to take the agro-chemical corporation to trial. Thousands of similar lawsuits are pending against the company and has brought national attention to the issue.

CHLORPYRIFOS – THE TOXIC PESTICIDE CURRENTLY HARMING OUR CHILDREN AND THE ENVIRONMENT

Scientists consider that the chemical chlorpyrifos has serious negative effects on our health – especially for children.

Exposure to it, even in small doses can impact on children's brain development. It has also been linked to developmental delays in children, memory loss and an increased risk of autism.

However, it is still widely used as a pesticide throughout Europe. In fact, it is one of the pesticides most commonly detected in fruits and vegetables across the continent. It's been found in soil and, in Spain, even in water.

Chlorpyrifos' current EU license expires in January 2019. Right now European authorities are reviewing the industry's renewal request for the pesticide.

PUBLIC PROTEST GETS RESULTS!

NEONICOTINOIDS

On 27 April 2018 the EU Commission announced a total ban on the use of the three most widely used neonicotinoids apart from use in closed greenhouses. However the ban does not cover similar pesticides such as sulfoxaflor so the risk to pollinators remains. The battle continues…!

For updates on these stories look at the website www.barbararustin.com

Acknowledgements

It is no secret that behind an author's first book there is often a supportive partner. Without Nigel's unstinting support and belief in the book, it would undoubtedly still be mouldering in a drawer. (Yes, even in these days of word-processors and clouds, there are still hard copies of early versions of *Bee Alert!* in drawers.)

Nor does the word 'support' do justice to the roles Nigel has played in ensuring *Bee Alert!* saw the light of day. He not only took up natural bee-keeping inspired by the book and helped me keep the book abreast of the very latest research but, in his role as sales and marketing guru, he has never doubted its sales potential.

I am grateful, too, to my sisters, Maxine and Claire, and all my friends who have followed the progress of *Bee Alert!*. First books generally take a while to complete as you learn your craft along the way. Some of you have followed its gestation with particular interest. Thanks to Diane and Dieter, Josepha, Simon and Susie, Roger, Vicky, Philippe, Barbara and Michael, and Larry and Barb. Three of them deserve special mention: Michael, a successful self-publisher, has been the most insistent in urging me on to the next step towards publication and Roger and Larry have shared their vast inside knowledge of the book industry from the retailing and publishing viewpoint respectively.

If you are fortunate, the unexpected bonus of writing a children's book is the people you meet on the way. I certainly struck lucky when I joined Faber's first ever Writing for Children Course. We were fortunate enough to have as our tutor Anthony McGowan. Tony has been unfailingly generous with advice and encouragement ever since. We have all continued to meet and honing my writing skills with this super-smart and multi-talented group over the years has been as entertaining as it has been enlightening. Tony and the Faberites – Allison, Beverley, Dan, Emma, Faye, Gita, Maria and Michelle – always saw the potential in *Bee Alert!* and, like Michael, continually urged me on.

As the story developed into a novel, Natascha Biebow gave very sound editorial advice. And, more recently, the wonderful Samantha Macintosh's vast publishing expertise and unquenchable enthusiasm about *Bee Alert!* have empowered me in the last push towards publication. Everyone should have a Sam in their life!

As a painter, and a lover of illustration since childhood, the appearance of this book was always going to be almost as important to me as the text. I was very lucky to first encounter Josephine Birch's work when she was doing a post-graduate course at the Royal Drawing School. Not only is she a highly talented artist and illustrator but a beekeeper too!

Chris Fraser, the book's designer, in marrying text and image in the most imaginative way, has also helped me to realize my dream that it should be a joy to handle and look at. Until I met her, I never knew of the 'secret' role book designers can play in enhancing the pleasure of reading a book. Chris has always gone the extra mile and taken this book way beyond my dreams.

Last, but certainly not least, an enormous thank you to all my children and my grandchildren for their encouragement.

Charles has been unfailingly interested in this as in all my endeavours, Sarah has always been exceedingly generous with her time and valuable publishing expertise whilst Charlotte, who is something of an expert on children's literature herself, has been incredibly perceptive in her advice. As first proof reader she has not only been meticulous but her insightful comments went way beyond the grammatical and typographical.

The Brighton brigade have cleverly managed always to be the right age to follow the book as it grew from a picture book to children's novel and, like their mother, Charlotte, have been generous with their enthusiasm and feedback. Thanks, in particular, to Samala and Isaac – perhaps my most faithful readers. Isaac, thanks, too, for checking that I knew the difference between a colon and a semi colon. It's true I have always been a bit casual about them.

All my grandchildren are a complete delight. Just the thought of them makes me smile. It was the wish to play a small part in protecting the environment for them, their peers and, in time, their own children that inspired this book.

Thank you one and all.

Bibliography/Books consulted

A World without Bees,
Alison Benjamin and Brian McCallum, Guardian Books, 2009

The Barefoot Beekeeper, P.J. Chandler, www.lulu.com

Bees, Their Vision, Chemical Senses and Language,
Karl von Frisch, Cornell University Press, 1971

The Dancing Bees, An Account of the Life and Senses of the Honey Bee,
Karl von Frisch, Methuen, 1954

The Life of the Bee, Maeterlinck, George Allen & Unwin, 1935

Fifty Years Among the Bees, C.C. Miller, Dover Publications, 2006

The Behaviour and Social Life of Bees, C.R. Ribbands, Dover Publications. 1964

The Buzz about Bees, Biology of a Superorganism, Jurgen Tautz, Springer, 2008

The Thinking Beekeeper, A Guide to Natural Beekeeping in Top Bar Hives,
Christy Hemenway, New Society Publishers, Canada, 2013

Useful Organisations for Further Information

Buglife, www.buglife.org.uk
Center for Food Safety, USA http://www.centerforfoodsafety.org
Friends of the Bees, www.friendsofthebees.org
Friends of the Earth, www.foe.co.uk
Natural Beekeeping, www.biobees.com
Pesticide Action Network, U.K. and Europe
Pesticides Forum, www.beyondpesticides.org
Soil Association, www.soilassociation.org

If you want to be part of the action

Consider joining (or asking your parents to join) one or more of these organisations. By signing their petitions on environmental issues, you will be making your voice heard and be able to influence government.

www.sumofus.org
www.avaaz.org
www.38degrees.org.uk